An Analysis of

Max Weber's

The Protestant Ethic and the Spirit of Capitalism

Sebastián G. Guzmán
with
James Hill

LONDON AND NEW YORK

Published by Macat International Ltd
24:13 Coda Centre, 189 Munster Road, London SW6 6AW.

Distributed exclusively by Routledge
4 Park Square, Milton Park, Abingdon, Oxon OX14 4RN
605 Third Avenue, New York, NY 10017

Routledge is an imprint of the Taylor & Francis Group, an informa business

www.macat.com
info@macat.com

Cataloguing in Publication Data
A catalogue record for this book is available from the British Library.
Library of Congress Cataloguing-in-Publication Data is available upon request.
Cover illustration: Etienne Gilfillan

ISBN 978-1-912303-82-3 (hardback)
ISBN 978-1-912127-26-9 (paperback)
ISBN 978-1-912282-70-8 (e-book)

Notice
The information in this book is designed to orientate readers of the work under analysis,
to elucidate and contextualise its key ideas and themes, and to aid in the development
of critical thinking skills. It is not meant to be used, nor should it be used, as a
substitute for original thinking or in place of original writing or research. References and
notes are provided for informational purposes and their presence does not constitute
endorsement of the information or opinions therein. This book is presented solely for
educational purposes. It is sold on the understanding that the publisher is not engaged
to provide any scholarly advice. The publisher has made every effort to ensure that
this book is accurate and up-to-date, but makes no warranties or representations with
regard to the completeness or reliability of the information it contains. The information
and the opinions provided herein are not guaranteed or warranted to produce particular
results and may not be suitable for students of every ability. The publisher shall not be
liable for any loss, damage or disruption arising from any errors or omissions, or from
the use of this book, including, but not limited to, special, incidental, consequential or
other damages caused, or alleged to have been caused, directly or indirectly, by the
information contained within.

CONTENTS

THE MACAT LIBRARY

The Macat Library is a series of unique academic explorations of seminal works in the humanities and social sciences – books and papers that have had a significant and widely recognised impact on their disciplines. It has been created to serve as much more than just a summary of what lies between the covers of a great book. It illuminates and explores the influences on, ideas of, and impact of that book. Our goal is to offer a learning resource that encourages critical thinking and fosters a better, deeper understanding of important ideas.

Each publication is divided into three Sections: Influences, Ideas, and Impact. Each Section has four Modules. These explore every important facet of the work, and the responses to it.

This Section-Module structure makes a Macat Library book easy to use, but it has another important feature. Because each Macat book is written to the same format, it is possible (and encouraged!) to cross-reference multiple Macat books along the same lines of inquiry or research. This allows the reader to open up interesting interdisciplinary pathways.

To further aid your reading, lists of glossary terms and people mentioned are included at the end of this book (these are indicated by an asterisk [*] throughout) – as well as a list of works cited.

Macat has worked with the University of Cambridge to identify the elements of critical thinking and understand the ways in which six different skills combine to enable effective thinking.
Three allow us to fully understand a problem; three more give us the tools to solve it. Together, these six skills make up the **PACIER** model of critical thinking. They are:

ANALYSIS – understanding how an argument is built
EVALUATION – exploring the strengths and weaknesses of an argument
INTERPRETATION – understanding issues of meaning

CREATIVE THINKING – coming up with new ideas and fresh connections
PROBLEM-SOLVING – producing strong solutions
REASONING – creating strong arguments

To find out more, visit **WWW.MACAT.COM.**

CRITICAL THINKING AND *THE PROTESTANT ETHIC AND THE SPIRIT OF CAPITALISM*

Primary critical thinking skill: ANALYSIS
Secondary critical thinking skill: REASONING

The German sociologist Max Weber is considered to be one of the founding fathers of sociology, and ranks among the most influential writers of the 20th-century. His most famous book, *The Protestant Ethic and the Spirit of Capitalism*, is a masterpiece of sociological analysis whose power is based on the construction of a rigorous, and intricately interlinked, piece of argumentation.

Weber's object was to examine the relationship between the development of capitalism and the different religious ideologies of Europe. While many other scholars focused on the material and instrumental causes of capitalism's emergence, Weber sought to demonstrate that different religious beliefs in fact played a significant role. In order to do this, he employed his analytical skills to understand the relationship between capitalism and religious ideology, carefully considering how far Protestant and secular capitalist ethics overlapped, and to what extent they mirrored each other.

One crucial element of Weber's work was his consideration the degree to which cultural values acted as implicit or hidden reasons reinforcing capitalist ethics and behavior – an investigation that he based on teasing out the 'arguments' that underpin capitalism. Incisive and insightful, Weber's analysis continues to resonate with scholars today.

ABOUT THE AUTHOR OF THE ORIGINAL WORK

Max Weber was born in Prussia in 1864 and is known as one of Germany's greatest political thinkers. He is also credited with helping found the discipline of sociology, and for his impressive economic work. Weber's reputation for thoughtfulness led to a career as a professor and editor, while his political knowledge and ideas were highly regarded, particularly during the turmoil that followed Germany's defeat in World War I. He co-founded the German Democratic Party and advised on the draft of the country's post-war constitution. Weber died of pneumonia in 1920, aged just 56.

ABOUT THE AUTHORS OF THE ANALYSIS

Sebastián G. Guzmán undertook his PhD research in sociology at the New School for Social Research in New York. He has taught at the Universidad Andrès Bello, Chile, and is currently Assistant Professor of Sociology at West Chester University of Pennsylvania.

James Hill did his postgraduate research in political economy at King's College London.

ABOUT MACAT

GREAT WORKS FOR CRITICAL THINKING

Macat is focused on making the ideas of the world's great thinkers accessible and comprehensible to everybody, everywhere, in ways that promote the development of enhanced critical thinking skills.

It works with leading academics from the world's top universities to produce new analyses that focus on the ideas and the impact of the most influential works ever written across a wide variety of academic disciplines. Each of the works that sit at the heart of its growing library is an enduring example of great thinking. But by setting them in context – and looking at the influences that shaped their authors, as well as the responses they provoked – Macat encourages readers to look at these classics and game-changers with fresh eyes. Readers learn to think, engage and challenge their ideas, rather than simply accepting them.

'Macat offers an amazing first-of-its-kind tool for interdisciplinary learning and research. Its focus on works that transformed their disciplines and its rigorous approach, drawing on the world's leading experts and educational institutions, opens up a world-class education to anyone.'

Andreas Schleicher
Director for Education and Skills, Organisation for Economic
Co-operation and Development

'Macat is taking on some of the major challenges in university education ... They have drawn together a strong team of active academics who are producing teaching materials that are novel in the breadth of their approach.'

Prof Lord Broers,
former Vice-Chancellor of the University of Cambridge

'The Macat vision is exceptionally exciting. It focuses upon new modes of learning which analyse and explain seminal texts which have profoundly influenced world thinking and so social and economic development. It promotes the kind of critical thinking which is essential for any society and economy. This is the learning of the future.'

Rt Hon Charles Clarke, former UK Secretary of State for Education

'The Macat analyses provide immediate access to the critical conversation surrounding the books that have shaped their respective discipline, which will make them an invaluable resource to all of those, students and teachers, working in the field.'

Professor William Tronzo, University of California at San Diego

WAYS IN TO THE TEXT

KEY POINTS

- A pioneer in the field of sociology* (the study of the history and functioning of society), Max Weber was born in 1864 in Prussia;* he wrote *The Protestant Ethic* after having a nervous breakdown.

- *The Protestant Ethic* argues that religious ideas help explain how societies form different economic and social structures.

- Critics consider *The Protestant Ethic* one of the classic works of twentieth-century sociology.

Who Was Max Weber?

The author of *The Protestant Ethic and the Spirit of Capitalism*, Max Weber was one of the founders of modern sociology; he remains one of the most important thinkers of the twentieth century. Born in 1864 in the city of Erfurt, near the center of modern Germany, Weber's academic training focused on the law. In his doctoral dissertation and "habilitation"* thesis (a degree following a PhD), he explored matters concerning both economic and legal history. By the time he was 30, Weber had been appointed a professor of economics at the University of Freiburg.* Two years later, he moved to the University of Heidelberg.*

In 1897, Weber suffered a nervous breakdown, which forced him to abandon teaching until 1902 and again from 1903 to 1919. About five years after his breakdown, Weber recovered enough to write *The Protestant Ethic*. The essay held great personal significance for Weber. He strongly identified with the ascetic*—self-denying—character of the lonely and self-reliant Puritans* he described; the Puritans were a sect* of the Protestant* branch of modern Christianity who believed that the Roman Catholic* influence should be removed from Christian worship. In his wife's words, this was the first work to "make Weber's star shine again" and "connected with the deepest roots of his personality."[1]

Weber, who began to work on the main themes of *The Protestant Ethic* in 1898, wrote the essay between 1903 and 1905. It first appeared in the journal *Archiv für Sozialwissenschaften und Sozialpolitik** (Archives for Social Science and Social Policy) in two separate issues in 1904 and 1905. In 1919, Weber revised *The Protestant Ethic*, adding extended footnotes to address his critics. The final version was published in book form in 1920. Thanks to *The Protestant Ethic*, Weber remains a key figure in twentieth-century thought.

What Does *The Protestant Ethic* Say?

Weber asked if certain Protestant beliefs were linked with capitalism* (the social and economic system dominant in the West today in which trade and industry are held in private hands and exercised for profit). This important question challenged the prevailing arguments of the time, suggesting that the features of capitalist societies came from preexisting economic conditions or material interests. Weber contended that ideas mattered too and were not subordinate to economic interests. He argued that we cannot trace the existence of a "spirit of capitalism"* simply to material or economic interests; because we can find this spirit only among certain groups, in certain regions and periods, we must examine other factors.

For Weber, the "spirit of capitalism" must, rather, be associated with the types of beliefs held by particular groups of people. He decided that the beliefs in question were most probably religious, since Roman Catholics and Protestants clearly diverged in their work ethics. Weber determined that Roman Catholics were less likely to be involved in business or the professions than Protestants. They were also generally less well-off than Protestants. He argued that this difference resulted from Roman Catholics' religiously based cultural orientation, which rendered them less suited to business than their Protestant neighbors.

Weber also noted that the capitalism of Western Europe and the United States was distinct from capitalism as practiced elsewhere in the world. Western capitalism retained specific characteristics: it organized free labor in a rational, calculated manner and pursued profit systematically. To understand the origins of capitalism, Weber argued, we should inquire about the origins of the "spirit" that guides it. Since this spirit seemed common among Protestants, Weber intended to find out if and how religious beliefs affected capitalism.

Weber suggested that some Protestant sects encouraged ascetic work—work conducted without concern for pleasure—for profit. These included the idea of work as a calling* as proposed by Martin Luther* (a vitally important figure in the founding of Protestant Christianity in the sixteenth century), and the Calvinist* idea of predestination.* "Calvinism" is a branch of Protestantism holding specific interpretations of certain Christian beliefs; "predestination" is the idea that God has already decided the course of events, notably who will make it to Heaven and who will not.

In both sects, individuals embraced work as way of demonstrating that they were "chosen" by God. Weber argued that this ethic had also become secular* (that is, nonreligious). This secularized version of the Protestant ethic had contributed to the rise of Western capitalism since the eighteenth century, when the doctrines of predestination and the virtue of ascetic work became popular.

Since the time of its publication, sociologists have both widely praised and criticized Weber's work. Authors proposing alternative theories about the origins of modern capitalism place themselves at the heart of a major debate when they confront the "Weber thesis." But while many claim the text is historically wrong and too imaginative, these criticisms have not affected the work's reputation. Rather, Weber's thought-provoking ideas and the original paths of research that they can inspire have made the work a classic.

Why Does *The Protestant Ethic* Matter?

The Protestant Ethic remains important for the originality of both its argument and its methodology. The work has become a foundational and highly influential piece in the discipline of sociology. Indeed, some may hold it as the most important piece. Scholars generally regarded it as a great exemplar of theoretically creative empirical* scholarship—that is, research capable of being verified or disproved through observation or experiment. It is hard to overstate the importance of Weber's thesis.

But the work does not remain relevant because of its historical accuracy; indeed, many disagree with Weber's analysis of history. It remains relevant because the development of modern capitalism has become a central issue in sociology. Other founders of the discipline, such as the nineteenth-century German political philosopher Karl Marx* and the pioneering French sociologist Émile Durkheim,* have also addressed this issue. Some see Weber's work as a critique of Marx's "historical materialist"* theory of industrial capitalism. Marx stressed the importance of material conditions in determining the economic and class structure of societies; Weber offered a counterpoint, making the case that ideas were significant also.

Beyond sociology, *The Protestant Ethic* has inspired important works in many other fields and subfields, such as the sociology of organizations.* This is the study of formal and informal institutions, influenced by Weber's analysis of bureaucracy;* its practitioners analyze the structure of these institutions and how these institutions determine the way individuals interact.

While some scholars still challenge the claims of *The Protestant Ethic*, sociologists today remain more concerned with using it to inspire new areas of research. The book has arguably become the most frequently cited source for ideas about the role that religious beliefs play in attitudes toward work—a fact that stems, naturally, from Weber's main thesis that the religious beliefs of certain Protestant sects could explain the development of modern capitalism. *The Protestant Ethic* has also become influential in the study of modernization and the rationalization* of society (that is, the move toward a social life governed by rational decisions and assumptions). Weber argues that the process of rationalization—particularly the rationalization of work—forms a distinctive part of the movement to modern capitalism.

NOTES

1 Marianne Weber, *Max Weber: A Biography*, trans. Harry Zohn (New Brunswick, NJ: Transaction Publishers, 1988), 335.

SECTION 1
INFLUENCES

MODULE 1
THE AUTHOR AND THE HISTORICAL CONTEXT

KEY POINTS

- A revolutionary text, *The Protestant Ethic* attempted to explain the development of modern capitalism.*
- Weber felt a great affinity with the asceticism*—the practice of self-denial—of the Puritans.*
- Weber sought to explain the development of modern capitalism at the start of the twentieth century.

Why Read *The Protestant Ethic*?

Max Weber's *The Protestant Ethic and the Spirit of Capitalism* remains one of the most important works of sociology* written in the twentieth century. Because Weber uses empirical* data to shape his argument (that is, data verifiable by observation), many believe the work has played a large role in establishing the academic discipline of sociology. Still, *The Protestant Ethic* remains relevant not just because of its methodological approach, but because of Weber's argument.

Weber asks why certain groups engage in different types of economic behavior. Two other founders of sociology, the political philosopher Karl Marx* and the French thinker Émile Durkheim,* had also engaged with this question. Weber argued that the ideas associated with certain religious groups determined economic behavior and the economic structure of societies. This directly critiqued Marx's "historical materialist"* theory, according to which material conditions shaped the economic organization of societies. Weber instead suggested that the role of ideas should not be neglected.

> ❝ Throughout his life Weber saw himself as a 'bourgeois scholar' with a sense of mission. ❞
>
> Kieran Allan, *Max Weber: A Critical Introduction*

Weber made a crucial and enduring contribution to scholarship by arguing that the beliefs of certain Protestant* groups could help explain the development of the economic and social system of modern capitalism.* While critics have challenged some of the empirical claims of *The Protestant Ethic* (that is, its scientific findings), it remains one of the most widely cited works discussing the role of ideas in the development of modern capitalism. As the British sociologist Anthony Giddens* comments: "*The Protestant Ethic and the Spirit of Capitalism* undoubtedly ranks as one of the most renowned, and controversial, works of modern social science."[1]

Author's Life

Max Weber was born in 1864 in Erfurt, Prussia* (a state incorporated into modern-day Germany and Poland) and died in 1920 in Munich, Germany. Weber had a tense relationship with his father, an important figure in German politics. His mother, very influenced by American Unitarianism* and English Progressive* Christianity (both strands of Protestant theology*), played a significant role in helping Weber develop his ideas about the Protestant ethic. Her activism in liberal religious circles inspired Weber to inquire about morality and made him aware of the role moral standards play in guiding an honorable life.

Although Weber's academic background centered primarily in the law, he wrote his doctoral thesis on economic and legal history. This led him to a career as a professor of economics—first at the University of Freiburg* in 1894 and then two years later at the University of Heidelberg.* After Weber's father died in 1897, he had a nervous breakdown that forced him to abandon teaching almost completely. He began to write *The Protestant Ethic* between 1903 and 1905. The highly influential journal *Archiv für Sozialwissenschaften und Sozialpolitik**2 published it in two separate issues in 1904 and 1905. In 1920, *The Protestant Ethic* was published in book form with extended footnotes addressing its critics.

The work had particular significance to Weber, who personally identified with the moral outlook of the Protestant groups he described. While other scholars might have arrived at the same arguments, Weber's personal connection to the concepts in *The Protestant Ethic* gave him important insights that other thinkers may have missed.

Author's Background

At the turn of the twentieth century, Germany (and many other parts of Europe) stood at a crossroads between its premodern* past and its modern present. Industrialization had not yet reached its countryside and villages, so in some ways the past remained on display. The cities, on the other hand, were rapidly industrializing. They represented modernity and the future. This divide inspired many studies of the period. Scholars asked how we could live and guide our lives under capitalism, which they saw as a system in which the market takes priority over tradition, ethical values, and personal relationships. In *The Protestant Ethic* Weber aimed in part to explain how modern capitalist society developed from more traditional forms of economic organization.

Another social issue of the period relevant to Weber's essay was discrimination (or the perception of discrimination). German Catholics, feeling they were underrepresented in civil-service jobs, lobbied for a quota system. Weber believed that Catholics held fewer business and professional jobs not because of discrimination but because of their religiously based cultural orientation. He saw Roman

Catholic culture as less suited to business than Protestant. The nineteenth-century French historian Alexis de Tocqueville* had suggested in his work *Democracy in America* that religion affected economic behavior.[3] But social scientists had not yet addressed the issue in a systematic manner. This practical problem motivated Weber to write an essay that contributed not only to the understanding of the social basis of economic life, as it is often understood today, but also to the policy debates of the period.

NOTES

1 Max Weber, *The Protestant Ethic and the Spirit of Capitalism*, trans. Talcott Parsons (London: Routledge, 2005), VII

2 *Archiv für Sozialwissenschaften und Sozialpolitik* (Archives for Social Science and Social Policy) was edited by Weber, Werner Sombart and Edgar Jaffé, and became the leading German journal of the time.

3 Victor Nee and Richard Swedburg, *On Capitalism* (Stanford, CA: Stanford University Press, 2007), 54.

ACADEMIC CONTEXT

KEY POINTS

- When Weber wrote *The Protestant Ethic*, one of the most important academic concerns involved exploring the development of modern capitalism.*

- At the time, arguments influenced by Marxist* scholarship dominated the discussion and the social analysis, emphasizing the role of material interests—class and economics—in the formation of society.

- Weber challenged these prevailing arguments, stressing the role of ideas and not just material interests.

The Protestant Ethic in its Context

German social scientists and historians of the period were very much interested in the origins of capitalism and the process of industrialization, and Max Weber's *The Protestant Ethic and the Spirit of Capitalism* was one of the most significant contributions to this line of inquiry.

When it came to political thought and economics, the intellectual environment in Germany differed sharply from that in Britain during the same period. Referencing the philosophical approaches of utilitarianism,* according to which an action is judged "right" according to its effect, and idealism,* according to which "reality" is a question of perception and thought, the British sociologist* Anthony Giddens* says: "The dominant position of utilitarianism and classical political economy in [Britain] were not reproduced in Germany, where these were held at arm's length by the influence of idealism and, in the closing decades of the nineteenth century, by the growing impact of Marxism."[1]

> **❝** [Weber] was a member of the so-called 'younger generation' associated with the Verein,* the first group to acquire a sophisticated knowledge of Marxist theory and to attempt to creatively employ elements drawn from Marxism—without ever accepting it as an overall system of thought, and recoiling from its revolutionary politics. **❞**
>
> Anthony Giddens, Introduction to *The Protestant Ethic*

The analytical approach of Karl Marx,* according to which material interests rather than *ideas*—religion and culture for example—determined the development of capitalism, was increasingly influential. But idealism remained the dominant methodology in Germany at the time; according to idealist principles human behavior could not simply be explained in terms of causal laws and instead "has to be 'interpreted' or 'understood' in a way which has no counterpart in nature."[2] This approach put a strong emphasis on the role of history in understanding human behavior because the "cultural values that lend meaning to human life … are created by specific processes of social development."[3]

Overview of the Field

Many of Weber's contemporaries regarded the Marxist economist and sociologist Werner Sombart* as one of the most important voices on the development of modern capitalism. Sombart coedited the journal that published Weber's *The Protestant Ethic*. He published his most significant work, *Der Moderne Kapitalismus* (*Modern Capitalism*), in 1902. In *The Protestant Ethic,* Weber directly engaged with Sombart's arguments in *Der Moderne Kapitalismus.*

Sombart used Karl Marx's materialist theory* of historical change to describe how capitalism evolved from its feudalist* roots (feudalism being a medieval social system in which, very broadly, land ownership dictated status and wealth). He divided the capitalist period into three different sections. Early capitalism ended just before the Industrial Revolution* took hold in the mid-eighteenth century. High capitalism began in the mid-eighteenth century. And late capitalism started at the dawn of World War I.* Sombart continued the debate in 1911 with *The Jews and Modern Capitalism* and *The Quintessence of Capitalism: A Study of the History and Psychology of the Modern Business Man* (1913).

Like many thinkers at the time, Sombart emphasized material interests over ideas as the main cause of modern capitalism in Germany and the rest of Europe. Beyond the academic debates, some common ideas suggested rudimentary versions of a Protestant ethic hypothesis— most notably the idea that religious beliefs affected work habits. Additionally, journalists and the educated public acknowledged a relationship between occupational status and religion. In a 1902 discussion of the relationship between the Protestant sect* of Calvinism* and the development of capitalism, Sombart commented that it was "too well-known a fact to require detailed explanation."[4] But social scientists had not studied this relationship in detail until Weber took up the challenge. Weber responded to Sombart—and to other critics—in extended footnotes to the 1920 book edition of *The Protestant Ethic*, as well as in other works.

Academic Influences

After moving to Heidelberg* in 1896, Weber met other important philosophers and social scientists. They became part of the so-called Weber circle, which included intellectuals such as Georg Jellinek,* Ernst Troeltsch* (both of whom influenced *The Protestant Ethic*), Werner Sombart, and the woman who would become Weber's wife— the sociologist and women's rights activist Marianne Weber.* Max Weber's influence also brought many other scholars to Heidelberg.

One of the most important of these was the now almost forgotten German economist and historian Eberhard Gothein.* While the Weber circle did not constitute a cohesive school of thought, some of its members significantly influenced *The Protestant Ethic*. In addition to Sombart, Weber also engaged with Edgar Jaffé,* another of his coeditors on the *Archiv für Sozialwissenschaft und Sozialpolitik*. Ernst Troeltsch guided Weber's secondary readings about the sociological implications of the Calvinist world view. Perhaps most importantly, Eberhard Gothein's *Economic History of the Black Forest* (1892) called Weber's attention to the role Calvinism played in the spread of capitalism. Yet Weber recalls that Jellinek's *The Declaration of the Rights of Man and Citizens* (1895) inspired him "to take up the study of Puritanism* once again."[5] Jellinek encouraged Weber to pay attention to the effects of religion—generally not the first place scholars of capitalism would look.

Other scholars who had an important influence on Weber, particularly in 1903 when he began to work on the epistemological* foundations of sociology (that is, the role of thought and ideas in the formation of society), were the neo-Kantians*—followers of the thought of the influential eighteenth-century German philosopher Immanuel Kant—and related intellectuals. The most notable of these were Heinrich Rickert,* Wilhelm Windelband,* Wilhelm Dilthey,* and Georg Simmel.* These philosophers distinguished between the human or cultural sciences and the positivist* natural sciences; for positivists, only knowledge that can be verified by experience is valid. Weber and Simmel developed an interpretative sociology,* or sociology of understanding (*verstehen*)—that stood in contrast to French positivist sociology. Rather than seeking to describe facts, it sought to explain the causes and consequences of actions by understanding the subjective *meaning* of actions—the meaning of work for Protestants, for example.

NOTES

1   Max Weber, *The Protestant Ethic and the Spirit of Capitalism*, trans. Talcott Parsons (London: Routledge, 2005), VIII.

2   Weber, *The Protestant Ethic and the Spirit of Capitalism*, IX.

3   Weber *The Protestant Ethic and the Spirit of Capitalism*, IX.

4   Max Weber, *Economy and Society: An Outline of Interpretive Sociology*, ed. Guenther Roth and Claus Wittich (Berkeley, CA: University of California Press, 1978), LXXVI.

5   Max Weber, *The Protestant Ethic and the "Spirit" of Capitalism: And Other Writings*, trans. Peter Baehr and Gordon C. Wells (New York: Penguin, 2002), 155.

MODULE 3
THE PROBLEM

KEY POINTS

- Academics in Weber's day focused on evaluating different factors associated with the development of modern capitalism.*

- The main arguments focused on material or rationalist* causes, as well as the roles of certain cultural groups.

- In *The Protestant Ethic*, Weber advanced an argument that the beliefs of certain Protestant* sects* had significant influence on the development of modern capitalism.

Core Question

In *The Protestant Ethic and the Spirit of Capitalism*, Max Weber sought to answer two core questions. The first was whether clear "elective affinities"* (a term denoting a kind of relationship or historical link) existed between certain Protestant beliefs and a "vocational* ethic" (roughly, a "work ethic"). Weber's precise focus here was whether or not there existed an affinity between the Protestant ethic and the "spirit of capitalism,"* by which he meant a way of organizing one's life around money, profit, and material success. This orientation toward work and economic gain did not exist in premodern economically "traditional" society: for a premodern culture work was a necessary evil, less valuable than leisure; people, then, were obliged to work only as required to meet traditional needs.

This core idea directly addressed the question of how modern capitalism had come to develop. Weber's argument rejected the materialist view of history* offered by Marxist*-influenced arguments, focusing on the role of economic interests. But Weber examined how

> **❝ The proverb says jokingly, 'either eat well or sleep well'. In the present case the Protestant prefers to eat well, the Catholic to sleep undisturbed. ❞**
> Max Weber, *The Protestant Ethic*

particular ideas held by certain groups could help explain the development of modern capitalism.

Weber's second question also related to the development of modern capitalism. He wondered "to what degree the historical origins of central features of our modern life can be attributed to religious forces stemming from the Reformation* [the events that led to the formation of the modern Protestant branch of Christianity in the sixteenth century] and to what degree to other forces."[1] The answer would provide an understanding of the origins of capitalism that addressed the monumental cultural change that capitalism represented, especially in light of people's modern orientation toward economic action.

The Participants

When Max Weber wrote *The Protestant Ethic*, the dominant literature in economic history denied that religion could influence an economic ethic. Traditional analysis held that modern capitalism stemmed from material interests and power, general evolution and progress, the business dealings of Jewish people, and abstract rationalism (the drive toward rational thought and behavior that defined modern societies), among other forces. Werner Sombart,* for example, stressed the role of Jews in the development of capitalism. He also held that capitalism represented one distinct stage in the rational development of societies. Others took Marx's work in another direction, seeing the development of capitalism in terms of class interests.

Economic historians tended not to focus systematically on interpreting the subjective "meanings" of economic action. Weber had not done this either in his own previous works. In fact, few professional historians discussed cultural history. The historian Eberhard Gothein*—who Weber had brought to Heidelberg* in 1904 to take over the chair in economic history he had vacated—remained one of the few exceptions to this rule. Gothein had floated the idea that the Protestant sect of Calvinism* helped spread capitalism; Weber extended this concept with a detailed analysis that specified the link between religious beliefs and capitalism from medieval Roman Catholicism* to the schism in the Christian religion known as the Reformation, and the theology* of Calvinism and the Protestant sects.

In doing this, *The Protestant Ethic* broke with the dominant literature in economic history; the work fitted well with the new discipline emerging in Germany: sociology.* The essay's focus on the interpretation of meanings became one of the foundations of the German tradition of "interpretative sociology,"* developed by Weber and the pioneering sociologist and philosopher Georg Simmel.*

The Contemporary Debate

In *The Protestant Ethic* Weber addressed many alternative theories of how modern capitalism had developed. He disagreed with Sombart's evolutionary thesis; indeed, that was one of Weber's main motivations for writing his essay. In contrast to Sombart, Weber suggested that changes do not develop in parallel in all spheres. Law emerged in the Middle Ages,* based on the principles of justice laid down in ancient Rome.* But modern capitalism developed in England, with a less rational form of law, the common law.* This undermines Sombart's argument.[2] Contrary to Marxist explanations, Weber claimed that the "spirit of capitalism" preceded the existence of a bourgeoisie (a middle class of business-owners) in the United States. In his view, capitalism was cultivated not so much by the commercial elite as by new entrepreneurs of middle-class origin. This analysis makes a simple class-based explanation of capitalism impossible.[3]

The Protestant Ethic received significant attention from thinkers in many disciplines. The most significant criticism came from the historians Felix Rachfahl* and H. Karl Fischer* who reviewed the essay in two journals, published in 1907 and 1909 respectively. Weber replied strongly to each of these reviews and to their authors' responses. He felt they lacked sufficient mastery of the topic to understand his work fully. Between 1911 and 1916, the economists Werner Sombart—also a sociologist—and Lujo Brentano* addressed *The Protestant Ethic* in larger works. Weber responded to them in extensive new footnotes to the 1920 book edition of *The Protestant Ethic*. While Weber clarified his arguments, he never changed any relevant ideas from those expressed in the original publication.

Sociologists both praised and criticized *The Protestant Ethic*. Beyond the discipline of sociology, scholars criticized it more often than praised it. These responses came from a wide range of disciplines, including history, economics, psychology, and even literary criticism. Many of the critics attacked the empirical* accuracy of Weber's arguments, such as his reading of the works of the American revolutionary Benjamin Franklin.*[4] Nevertheless, authors proposing alternative theories about the origins of modern capitalism were forced to confront the "Weber thesis" if they wished to place themselves at the core of a major debate.

NOTES

1   Weber, *The Protestant Ethic and the Spirit of Capitalism: With Other Writings on the Rise of the West*, trans. Stephen Kalberg, 4th ed. (New York: Oxford University Press, 2009), XXVIII.

2   Fritz Ringer, *Max Weber: An Intellectual Biography* (Chicago: University of Chicago Press, 2010), 117.

3   Ringer, *Max Weber*, 115.

4   Ringer, *Max Weber*, 125.

THE AUTHOR'S CONTRIBUTION

KEY POINTS

- Weber argued that religious ideas could help explain the development of the economic and social system of modern capitalism* through their effect on economic behavior.

- While some had written on this subject before Weber, he was the first thinker to link religious ideas to an explanation of modern capitalism.

- Weber wrote in response to the work of the Marxist* economist and sociologist* Walter Sombart,* and built upon the work of the philosopher of law Georg Jellinek* and the cultural historian Eberhard Gothein,* respectively.

Author's Aims

In writing *The Protestant Ethic and the Spirit of Capitalism*, Max Weber was motivated by skepticism about existing explanations of how modern capitalism developed. These explanations tended to treat cultural values "as passive forces generally subordinate to social structures, power, classes, evolution and progress, and economic and political interests."[1] Walter Sombart notably made this argument in his work *Der Moderne Kapitalismus* (1902). Weber also had great reservations about narratives that placed a few great individuals as the drivers of history.

Weber also attempted to explain the specific form Western capitalism had taken in terms of the "spirit of capitalism."* As Weber saw it, Western capitalism organized labor in a rational and calculated manner to better pursue profit. He suggested that the "spirit of capitalism" contributed to this by serving as a secular* "ethically

> 66 The fate of our times is characterised by rationalisation and intellectualisation and, above all, by the 'disenchantment of the world'. 99
>
> Max Weber, "Science as a Vocation"

oriented maxim" for the systematic "organization of life" around money, profit, work, competition, and material success as ends in themselves.[2] To understand the origins of capitalism, Weber felt we should examine the origins of its spirit. This spirit seemed prevalent among Protestants.* So Weber remained particularly interested in finding out whether and how religious beliefs could produce this spirit.

Approach

In determining how modern capitalism developed, Weber examined how cultural values could determine the economic structure of societies—a kind of inquiry previously undertaken only at the margins of academia. Weber investigated the motivation for certain behaviors in large groups of people, wanting to uncover the "subjective meaning of social action." This became a central feature of his approach to historical interpretation throughout his work. By developing this interpretative sociology,* or sociology of understanding (*verstehen*), Weber rejected the approaches of positivism* and economic determinism* to understanding social phenomena. For positivists, only knowledge that could be verified by experience was valid; economic determinism holds that economic relationships are fundamental to explaining social phenomena (an idea associated with classic Marxist thought).

Weber became one of the first thinkers to explain the differences in economic behavior between Protestants and Roman Catholics. He did this by examining the meaning behind the actions of Protestant and Roman Catholic behavior and their religious origins. He argued that preexisting material conditions could not explain the economic choices prevalent in some regions within Germany; they could not explain, for example, why Protestants were generally wealthier than Roman Catholics.[3] Nor could they explain why Roman Catholics tended to study subjects in the humanities* rather than the business-oriented curriculum Protestants favored. It seemed clear to Weber that religious beliefs played an important role in determining people's economic behaviors; this, he believed, deserved serious investigation. His line of inquiry challenged the orthodoxy of the Marxist-influenced theories popular at the time, according to which material matters (economics, chiefly) were paramount in shaping society.

Contribution in Context

The idea of a causal link between Protestantism and capitalism diverged from mainstream scholarship of the time. It did not originate with Weber, however; he notes that the Spanish saw a link between Dutch Calvinism* and the promotion of trade. The British economist Sir William Petty* made a similar claim.[4] The economic historian Eberhard Gothein's* depiction of the Calvinist diaspora*—the international spread of Calvinists—as the "seed bed of capitalist economy"[5] heavily influenced Weber's research.

Weber also wrote in reaction to the work of Werner Sombart. In *Der Moderne Kapitalismus* (1902), Sombart argued that material conditions within capitalism created certain ideas within Protestant sects.*[6] Weber, however, felt that Sombart got the cause and the consequence confused: for Weber, modern capitalism stemmed from "the spirit of capitalism" found within some elements of Protestantism. Another early writer who focused on the effect religion had on the structure of capitalism was the philosopher of law Georg Jellinek.* Weber's focus on Puritanism* resulted directly from the ideas Jellinek expressed in *The Declaration of the Rights of Man and Citizens* (1895).

Jellinek, Sombart, Gothein, and others were part of what became known as the "Weber circle." While not a school of thought in its own right, many of its members contributed to Weber's thinking about the development of modern capitalism.

NOTES

1   Max Weber, *The Protestant Ethic and the Spirit of Capitalism: With Other Writings on the Rise of the West*, trans. Stephen Kalberg, 4th ed. (New York: Oxford University Press, 2009), xxv–vi.

2   Weber, *The Protestant Ethic and the Spirit of Capitalism: With Other Writings on the Rise of the West*, 17.

3   Max Weber, *The Protestant Ethic and the Spirit of Capitalism*, trans. Talcott Parsons (London: Routledge, 2005), 4

4   Weber, *The Protestant Ethic and the Spirit of Capitalism*, 10

5   Weber, *The Protestant Ethic and the Spirit of Capitalism*, 10

6   Werner Sombart, *Der Moderne Kapitalismus* "Modern Capitalism: A Historical and Systematic Exposition of Europe's Economic Life from Its Beginnings to the Present Day." No English translation is available.

SECTION 2
IDEAS

MAIN IDEAS

KEY POINTS

- The key themes Weber addresses include the origins of the "spirit of capitalism"* within certain Protestant* sects* and how some religious ideas can explain the development of modern capitalism.*

- Weber argues that we can explain rationalized,* secular,* "modern" capitalism by looking at how the ideas of the Lutheran* and Calvinist* sects encouraged people to act.

- The first part of *The Protestant Ethic* explains the problem and the second analyzes it.

Key Themes

Weber begins his argument in *The Protestant Ethic and the Spirit of Capitalism* by observing that Protestants tended to be wealthier and more often involved in business than Roman Catholics.* He notes that "business leaders and owners of capital, as well as the higher grades of skilled labour, and even more the higher technically and commercially trained personnel of modern enterprises, are overwhelmingly Protestant."[1] This led Weber to his main hypothesis. He argued that something in the religious beliefs of Protestants—especially Calvinists and the followers of the German priest Martin Luther,* a key figure in the schism in the Christian religion that led to the founding of the religion's Protestant branch—led them to develop an economic ethic highly compatible with capitalist production.

The economic ethic of systematic work and the rational pursuit of profit has not existed everywhere or at all times. But it appeared in the West somewhat before the development of modern capitalism. To

> ❝ The modern man is in general, even with the best will, unable to give religious ideas a significance for culture and national character which they deserve. But one can, of course, not aim to replace a one-sided materialistic with an equally one-sided spiritualistic causal interpretation of culture and of history. ❞
>
> Max Weber, *The Protestant Ethic*

Weber this suggests that the "spirit of capitalism" has potentially played a role in sparking the development of modern capitalism.

Weber describes the conceptual foundations of "the spirit of capitalism" in Calvinism and other Protestant sects. He looks at John Calvin's* doctrine of predestination;* Calvin, a sixteenth-century French theologian,* taught that some people were destined to go to heaven and others—despite anything they might do in their lifetimes—would not. He argues that this created an unbearable despair among the devout: "a feeling of unprecedented inner loneliness of the single individual."[2] However, Calvinist theologians (scholars of religious thought and scripture) later revised the doctrine: believers who organized their life around methodical ascetic* work (work requiring self-denial) in a calling* and the pursuit of profit might enter heaven after all. This produced great psychological rewards for the faithful.

The sixteenth-century German cleric Martin Luther introduced the concept of a calling, claiming "every person had a 'calling' or 'vocation' given to him or her by God."[3] Weber believes this explains why Protestants remained more likely to be wealthy and to pursue a career in business.

Weber concluded his argument by explaining the historical link between the Protestant ethic and capitalism in more general terms. He argues that the ethos of ascetic work spread in the colonies that would become the United States in the eighteenth century. But in this new country it became secularized. Capitalism no longer needed the religious foundations of the spirit to reproduce itself: after society moved toward a rational basis, each individual would have no choice but to embrace capitalism: "Profit was now sought not to ensure one's state of grace, but because it was in one's self-interest to do so."[4]

Exploring the Ideas

The Protestant Ethic contains three original and connected ideas. First, the importance of the "spirit" of modern capitalism and its origins in the Protestant ethic. Second, Luther's idea of work as a calling, and how Calvinist interpretations of the relationship between predestination and the calling motivated ascetic work in the pursuit of profit. Third, the secularized version of the Protestant ethic that had developed since the eighteenth century, especially in America. This sequence of ideas forms the core of the so-called "Weber thesis": the Protestant ethic created the orientation to work necessary for modern capitalism to develop, but today the explicit religious connection has been largely severed.

Without this work ethic contained in the "spirit of capitalism," Weber believes workers would only be motivated to work as much as necessary to satisfy traditional needs.[5] The origins of the Protestant ethic lie in Luther's idea of vocational* work as a calling: "labour in everyday life was seen as a God appointed task."[6] Luther's "this-worldly work" contrasted with the ascetic withdrawal from the world of Roman Catholic monks.

Those who adopted the ascetic ethic of Calvinism and the Protestant sects developed a closer "inner affinity"* with capitalism. They exalted success in the calling and in intensified labor. John Calvin's initial doctrine of predestination caused insufferable anguish among the faithful. But those who behaved in a manner that suggested they had been chosen, by embracing their calling, reaped significant psychological rewards from ascetic work. Other scholars before Weber had mentioned a relationship between Calvinism and capitalism. But they had not offered specific details of linkage.

In the eighteenth century, the ethos of ascetic work grew in the United States, but in a secularized fashion. The work, business, and ethics of American revolutionary politician Benjamin Franklin* offer a clear example of this. Franklin advised, for example, that "time is money"[7] and emphasized the importance of acting justly in financial affairs: "Remember this saying, *The good paymaster is lord of another man's purse.*"[8] Ascetic work and wealth no longer earned a person's salvation. Instead they demonstrated good moral character and were values a community-oriented citizen should possess. Weber concluded that in revolutionary-era America, "victorious capitalism" no longer needed the idea of work as a calling to reproduce itself. Once a significant number of entrepreneurs organized their production in a modern capitalistic manner, competition would force the rest to follow or perish.

Scholars have used Weber's ideas to call attention to the importance of the cultural—and especially religious—foundations of orientations and motivations to work. His ideas have also illustrated the relationship between Protestantism and capitalism and, more broadly, rationalism.* The concept of rationalization* (the process in which actions calculated to achieve a given end are increasingly adopted) has been used to explain how social behaviors originally influenced by religious teachings can continue in secular societies.

Language and Expression

Weber targeted *The Protestant Ethic* at German social scientists and historians who fueled the academic debate about the origins of capitalism and industrialism. Because he did not aim to attract a lay audience, Weber writes in an academic style often using specialized language. For example, instead of using the words "free will," Weber instead uses the Latin phrase *liberum arbitrium*. The work is not, however, difficult to understand. His use of particular phrases perhaps relates to when the work was written, rather than the audience he aimed to reach.

Weber organized *The Protestant Ethic* into two straightforward parts. The briefer first part explains the research problem and its relevance. Part Two contains the analytic core and Weber's conclusions.

Weber's famous use of the term "iron cage"* was first found in a 1930 English translation of *The Protestant Ethic* made by the sociologist* Talcott Parsons.* Weber used the German term "*stahlhartes Gehäuse*," or "iron cage," to describe the increasing rationalization of social and economic life in Western society. Some critics have argued, however, that rather than "iron cage," a more accurate translation may be "steel-hard casing."[9]

NOTES

1   Max Weber, *The Protestant Ethic and the Spirit of Capitalism*, trans. Talcott Parsons (London: Routledge, 2005), 3.

2   Weber, *The Protestant Ethic and the Spirit of Capitalism*, 60.

3   Kieran Allen, *Max Weber: A Critical Introduction* (Pluto Press, 2004), 36.

4   Laura Desfor Edles and Scott Appelrouth, *Sociological Theory in the Classical Era: Text and Readings*, 3rd ed. (Thousand Oaks, CA: Sage, 2014), 166.

5   Weber, *The Protestant Ethic and the Spirit of Capitalism*, 24.

6   Allen, *Max Weber*, 36.

7   Weber, *The Protestant Ethic and the Spirit of Capitalism*, 14.

8   Weber, *The Protestant Ethic and the Spirit of Capitalism*, 15.

9   Peter Baehr, "The 'Iron Cage' and the 'Shell as Hard as Steel': Parsons, Weber, and the Stahlhartes Gehäuse Metaphor in the Protestant Ethic and the Spirit of Capitalism," *History and Theory* 40, no. 2 (2001): 153–69.

MODULE 6
SECONDARY IDEAS

KEY POINTS

- Weber's arguments have helped scholars criticize theories of history, such as those of Karl Marx,* founded on the role of material circumstances; they have contributed to cultural theories of economic development, and explained the role of the religious doctrine of predestination* in the development of capitalism.*

- Weber's work helped undermine the dominant Marxist* theories of his day.

- Weber's argument about the doctrine of predestination and the development of modern capitalism has had the greatest impact. This is thanks to its fundamental importance for the whole "Weber thesis."

Other Ideas

Max Weber supports each of his primary ideas in *The Protestant Ethic and the Spirit of Capitalism* with a series of secondary ideas. Many of these have influenced sociological* thought significantly. Weber claimed that capitalism itself could not have created the "spirit of capitalism."* Scholars have used this notion to argue against historical materialist* concepts, such as those of Karl Marx, with their emphasis on economic matters over ideas. Weber adds that even if capitalism could help to spread the "spirit," some force had to develop and sustain the idea that systematic pursuit of profit was desirable. The idea had to have a group, organization or class to serve as "social carriers."[1] That phrase is another influential concept Weber developed.

Weber argues that preexisting differences in the groups' material wealth cannot completely explain differences in economic attainment

> **❝** We can clearly identify the traces of the influence of the doctrine of predestination in the elementary forms of conduct and attitude toward life in the era with which we are concerned, even where its authority as a dogma was on the decline. **❞**
>
> Max Weber, *The Protestant Ethic*

between Protestants* and Roman Catholics.* This notion influenced culturalist* explanations of inequality and poverty—explanations that seek to explain material circumstances by looking at the role of culture; some argue, for example, that understanding different cultural attitudes toward economic behavior can help us account for differences in development throughout the world.[2] The German economist Sascha O. Becker* suggested that Weber's analysis of Protestant and Roman Catholic attitudes can even help explain contemporary economic problems in the eurozone* (the parts of Europe in which the euro is the currency).[3] Generally Protestant northern European countries exhibit more financial prudence than Roman Catholic Mediterranean countries. According to this view, cultural attitudes determine these countries' varying economic situations. When these attitudes clash, political crises ensue.

Exploring the Ideas

The most important secondary idea Weber raises involves the sociological effects surrounding the concept of salvation (the Christian doctrine according to which God saves the worthy from eternal damnation), especially its material consequences. This became a central element in Weber's subsequent works in the sociology of religion, which have remained influential. He traces how Roman Catholics, Lutherans,* Calvinists,* and the other sects* of the Protestant branch of Christianity dealt with the problem of salvation.

Catholics believe that sins can be forgiven in confession, allowing even former sinners to attain salvation. But Protestant sects took a harder line on sin—especially the Calvinists, who preached predestination (according to which the fate of the individual's soul is entirely decided by God). So how could they ease the anxieties of the faithful worried about salvation? They turned to the notion of rational work as a calling*—a God-given task. This gave religious meaning to work previously considered mundane.

Calvin's "doctrine of predestination" produced widespread hopelessness among believers, since they could not know or control the eventual fate of their soul. So theologians* and ministers of later Christian sects, among them the Pietist,* Methodist,* Quaker,* and Baptist* sects, reinterpreted the doctrine. Saved people, they suggested, exhibited four major qualities: first, the capacity for methodical work; second, the ability to create wealth and profit; third, becoming holy (or conducting themselves virtuously); fourth, feeling that they are possessed by God.[4] These signs offered great comfort to those who organized their life through methodical ascetic* work.

The British sociologist Ken Morrison explains how this created a "tendency among Protestants to distance themselves from the world."[5] A Protestant walked a solitary, God-given path to salvation. No outside influences could change this.[6] Furthermore, the ascetic approach to work put a "'psychological premium' on the regulation of one's own life that influenced the development of capitalism as a form of economic conduct."[7] So Calvin's doctrine not only affected the behavior of those who followed. It also established the conditions in which modern capitalism would develop.

Overlooked

Max Weber's *The Protestant Ethic* remains one of the most widely discussed works in the social sciences. It is hard to think of an aspect of the text that has not received attention. Scholars have extensively scrutinized its central and secondary arguments. And many of its ideas have inspired research in completely different areas. Scholars seem to have explored virtually all of the work's possible applications.

Nevertheless, some ideas have received more attention than Weber might have expected, and are attaining new significance. The most notable example is the metaphor that rationalization* of Western capitalism has constructed an "iron cage" in which individuals live. The influential sociologist Talcott Parsons* coined the term in his 1930 translation of the book; the first to be published in English, it has since become classic. Recent translators have criticized his word choice, however; for them, Weber's phrase "*stahlhartes Gehäuse*" may be more accurately translated as "steel-hard casing"[8] or "shell as hard as steel."[9] Nevertheless, Parsons's concept has achieved a special significance and resonance of its own, largely independent of the context in which Weber used the metaphor. It appears in the title of hundreds of sociological works, and scholars often apply it to rather unrelated topics, such as organizational analysis.[10]

NOTES

1   Max Weber, *The Protestant Ethic and the Spirit of Capitalism: With Other Writings on the Rise of the West*, trans. Stephen Kalberg, 4th ed. (New York: Oxford University Press, 2009), LIII.

2   Lawrence E. Harrison and Samuel P. Huntington, *Culture Matters: How Values Shape Human Progress* (New York: Basic Books, 2000).

3   Chris Arnot, "Protestant v Catholic: Which Countries Are More Successful?" *Guardian*, October 31, 2011, accessed September 5, 2015, http://www.theguardian.com/education/2011/oct/31/economics-religion-research

4   Weber, *The Protestant Ethic and the Spirit of Capitalism: With Other Writings on the Rise of the West*, XXXV

5   Ken Morrison, *Marx, Durkheim, Weber: Formations of Modern Social Thought* (Sage, 2006), 322.

6   Morrison, *Marx, Durkheim, Weber*, 322.

7   Morrison, *Marx, Durkheim, Weber*, 324.

8   Weber, *The Protestant Ethic and the Spirit of Capitalism: With Other Writings on the Rise of the West*, 158.

9   Max Weber, *The Protestant Ethic and the "Spirit" of Capitalism: And Other Writings*, trans. Peter Baehr and Gordon C. Wells (New York: Penguin, 2002), 121.

10 James R. Barker, "Tightening the Iron Cage: Concertive Control in Self-Managing Teams," *Administrative Science Quarterly* 38, no. 3 (1993): 408–37.

ACHIEVEMENT

KEY POINTS

- *The Protestant Ethic* deeply influenced the establishment of the field of sociology.*

- Weber's empirical* approach gave weight to his original thesis demonstrating the effect of religious beliefs on economic behavior.

- Weber's argument may look less secure today because modern researchers have access to more—and different—sources of empirical data than Weber did at the turn of the twentieth century.

Assessing the Argument

With its highly original argument, Max Weber's *The Protestant Ethic and the Spirit of Capitalism* remains one of the most debated and celebrated works in the social sciences. Indeed, scholars consider it one of the foundational works in the discipline of sociology and a great example of empirical sociological research. Nevertheless, some might suggest that Weber did not achieve all he set out to do and many scholars have criticized the evidence that forms the basis of the "Weber thesis." For example, the German economists Sascha O. Becker* and Ludger Woessmann* argue that Protestant* economic success did not stem from the Protestant work ethic; for them, it can be explained by the much higher literacy rate among Protestants.[1] But, in Weber's defense, modern academics such as Becker and Woessmann have access to much more data than Weber did in his day.

But we cannot determine *The Protestant Ethic*'s contribution to scholarship solely by the accuracy of its empirical work. It remains

> **❝** *The Protestant Ethic and the Spirit of Capitalism*
> written in 1904–5, is probably the most important
> sociological work of the twentieth century. **❞**
> Daniel Bell, review of *The Protestant Ethic*

important because of its contribution to the debate about the development of modern capitalism* in Germany, Western Europe more broadly, and the United States. Weber criticized Karl Marx's* influential argument that material (principally economic) factors were the primary engine for historical progress. Weber demonstrated that history had no rules, taking on an idea with many important adherents.

Achievement in Context

The influential journal *Archiv für Sozialwissenschaften und Sozialpolitik** (Archives for Social Science and Social Policy) published *The Protestant Ethic* in a series of journal articles in 1904 and 1905. Weber served as a coeditor of this journal, along with his sometime critic the Marxist economist and sociologist Wermer Sombart.* As it was one of the most famous and prestigious journals in Germany, Weber's work reached its intended audience with no difficulty. While *The Protestant Ethic* was only available in German until Talcott Parsons* translated it in 1930, meaning that English-speakers had to wait 25 years to access the work, the delay seems to have had little effect on its status.

Any empirical argument will be open to dispute when new evidence surfaces. For example, the Italian German economist Davide Cantoni* has argued that Protestantism and economic growth have no relationship: "Using population figures of 272 cities in the years 1300–1900, I find no effects of Protestantism on economic growth. The finding is precisely estimated, robust to the inclusion of various controls, and does not depend on data selection or small sample size."[2] But others claim evidence exists to support Weber's thesis. The economists Ulrich Blum* and Leonard Dudley* claim that between 1500 and 1750, wages fell in Roman Catholic* cities and increased in Protestant ones.[3] Nevertheless, the scholarly value of *The Protestant Ethic* does not rest solely on the accuracy of its empirical arguments.

Limitations

One of Weber's motivations in writing *The Protestant Ethic* was to understand and explain the roots of Western rationalization* (the process by which social behavior comes to be governed by rational decisions and behavior). Weber explained that the process of "rationalization in the West was advanced by a process he called calculation."[4] This meant that as economic values began to play a larger role in everyday life, assigning monetary values to things offered people greater control of the material world.[5] Weber used the process of rationalization to explain the specific form of capitalism that emerged in Western Europe and the United States. In this sense we might argue that *The Protestant Ethic* only helps us analyze the economic conditions of Western Europe and the United States.

While Weber certainly argues that the Protestant ethic acted as a catalyst for the development of modern capitalism, he does not suggest that it is the only catalyst. As such, *The Protestant Ethic* has relevance beyond Europe and the United States because it raises the question of the potential link between religion and economic behavior. Weber addressed the issue in his major research project "Economic Ethics of the World Religions"[6]—with additional discussion in *Economy and Society* (1921)[7] and *General Economic History* (1923). Most notably, he analyzed why modern capitalism did not emerge in India or China. He looked at the role of religion and economic ethics, as well as material conditions, the law and the judicial system, among other factors.

Nevertheless, some scholars such as James Blaut,* an American professor of anthropology* and geography, have criticized Weber's ideas as Eurocentric* (that is, assuming the primacy of European experience and perspectives). In his view, Weber subscribes to a view of European exceptionalism—the belief that Europe is somehow a "special case"—that overestimates the uniqueness of Western rationalism* or of the "spirit of capitalism."[8] Scholars have also criticized Weber for attributing to other cultures a propensity for economic backwardness. As many of his time did, he overlooked or undervalued non-Western elements of the culture. He did not account for the fact that European colonialism had oppressed some native cultures.

NOTES

1   Sascha O. Becker and Ludger Woessmann, "Was Weber Wrong? A Human Capital Theory of Protestant Economic History," Program on Education Policy and Governance, Harvard University (2007).

2   Davide Cantoni, "The Economic Effects of the Protestant Reformation: Testing the Weber Hypothesis in the German Lands," *Journal of the European Economic Association* 13, no. 4 (2014): 561.

3   Ulrich Blum and Leonard Dudley, "Religion and Economic Growth: Was Weber Right?" *Journal of Evolutionary Economics* 11, no. 2 (2001): 207–30.

4   Ken Morrison, *Marx, Durkheim, Weber: Formations of Modern Social Thought* (London: Sage, 2006), 284.

5   Morrison, *Marx, Durkheim, Weber*, 284–5.

6   This was a major project that Weber worked on mainly between 1911 and 1914, but which he completed in 1920 with the German publication of his *Collected Essays in the Sociology of Religion*. Among the main works here are *The Protestant Ethic*, *The Religion of China* (1915), *The Religion of India* (1916), *Ancient Judaism* (1917), and the "Introduction to the Economic Ethics of the World Religions" (1920).

7   Max Weber, *Economy and Society: An Outline of Interpretive Sociology*, ed. Guenther Roth and Claus Wittich (Berkeley: University of California Press, 1978).

8   J. M. Blaut, *Eight Eurocentric Historians* (New York: Guilford Press, 2000), 29.

PLACE IN THE AUTHOR'S WORK

KEY POINTS

- Weber's life's work involved investigating the development of Western capitalism.*

- *The Protestant Ethic* was Weber's first attempt to explain this development.

- *The Protestant Ethic* established Weber as one of the most influential thinkers of the twentieth century.

Positioning

The Protestant Ethic and the Spirit of Capitalism represents the first major piece in Max Weber's mature phase of production. In this period, and after his recovery from a nervous breakdown, he turned toward interpretative sociology:* an approach to the field that, rather than focusing on describing facts, seeks to explain the causes and consequences of actions by understanding their subjective *meaning*. After publication of *The Protestant Ethic* in 1905, Weber continued to investigate the effects of religion on economic behavior and social structure in his article "The Protestant Sects and the Spirit of Capitalism" (1906). Inspired by his 1904 trip to the United States, the article analyzed the relation between Protestantism* and capitalism in that country at the turn of the twentieth century.

Weber noted that in the United States, Protestantism encouraged the development of capitalism. He attributed this to psychological inducements connected with the concept of predestination* created by the beliefs held by certain Protestant sects* (that is to say, he argues that people acted as if they were chosen because this made life more bearable.) But these inducements also existed in Europe. In the United

States, Weber argued, Protestant churches also created a certain group discipline that reinforced moral economic behavior favoring capitalist development. These disciplines included paying debts on time and charging fair prices. Weber saw this behavior in the United States as paving the way for the capitalist spirit to transform into a secular* work ethic; eventually, this work ethic encompassed the whole of society and was not limited to certain Protestant sects.

With his essay on the Protestant sects in the United States, Weber began to extend his original argument. First, he moved beyond an analysis of Christian religions, broadening the scope of his comparative work. In his project "Economic Ethics of the World Religions," developed between 1911 and 1914,[1] looking at non-Western religions including Hinduism,* Buddhism,* Confucianism,* Taoism,* and Judaism* (a religion with its roots in the Middle East), Weber examined how each shaped the way their believers related to economic issues. To him, this explained why capitalism did not develop outside the West, notably in India and China.

Integration

After publication of *The Protestant Ethic*, Weber began to focus on other factors that could cause the development of capitalism and the process of Western rationalization.* He did not suggest that religion can explain everything relating to the development of modern capitalism. Instead, he emphasized that material conditions also had an important role to play. Weber developed his research on the rise of Western capitalism in both *Economy and Society* (1921) and *General Economic History* (1923).

He argued that other factors also played a role in the development of Western capitalism. These included rational accounting* methods and price-setting to generate profit, and a system of law with calculable results. All of these developed in the West at roughly the same time as capitalism. Comparing the West to other regions across the globe further highlighted the importance of these nonreligious factors. For instance, Weber noted that the lack of "formally guaranteed law and a rational administration and judiciary" in China created obstacles to capitalist development.[2]

Analyzing the role of religion and other factors in the unique development of rational capitalist economic organization in the West might seem an ambitious project. But Weber did not stop there. He became involved in even more ambitious research, focusing on the rise of rationality in Western culture. In this he included the development of the capitalist economy, formal, rational law, and the bureaucratic* state.

As for how *The Protestant Ethic* fits with Weber's broader concerns, the British sociologist Ken Morrison notes, "Some of the shortcomings in Weber's overall body of works meant that his writings as a whole have generally not been viewed as a unified body of work organized as a complete thematic whole."[3] Indeed, commentators such as the German sociologist Friedrich Tenbruck have argued that it is difficult to find any thematic unity throughout Weber's work.[4]

Significance

The Protestant Ethic stands as a major piece in Weber's impressive and influential body of work on the development of Western capitalism and its unique form of rationalism.* Many scholars feel that Weber's arguments in *The Protestant Ethic* remain open to criticism. But few deny the importance of his contribution to the debate around the development of modern capitalism—and the ingenuity of his approach.

Weber's first attempt to systematically explain the roots of modern capitalist society, *The Protestant Ethic*, remains his best-known work. Ken Morrison suggests "it was viewed as a classic as soon as it was published."[5] Largely because of the originality of his argument, the work also helped Weber establish his reputation as one of the founders of the discipline of sociology. As the sociologist Kieran Allen indicates, *The Protestant Ethic* "is regarded by many sociologists as one of the key texts in their discipline."[6] Weber's empirical* approach involved careful and detailed historical research. This novel manner of working shaped the way sociological research is conducted today. The publication, and later the translation, of *The Protestant Ethic* established Weber as one of the most important thinkers of the twentieth century. This reputation has not diminished.

NOTES

1   This was a major project that Weber worked on mainly between 1911 and 1914, but which he never completed; however, the 1920 German publication of his *Collected Essays in the Sociology of Religion* provides an insight into Weber's ideas. Among the main works here are *The Protestant Ethic*, *The Religion of China* (1915), *The Religion of India* (1916), *Ancient Judaism* (1917), and the "Introduction to the Economic Ethics of the World Religions" (1920).

2   Max Weber, *The Religion of China: Confucianism and Taoism*, trans. Hans H. Gerth (New York: Free Press, 1951), 85.

3   Ken Morrison, *Marx, Durkheim, Weber: Formations of Modern Social Thought* (London: Sage, 2006), 275.

4   Friedrich H. Tenbruck, "The Problem of Thematic Unity in the Works of Max Weber," *British Journal of Sociology* 31, no. 3 (1980): 316–51.

5   Morrison, *Marx, Durkheim, Weber*, 313.

6   Kieran Allen, *Max Weber: A Critical Introduction* (Pluto Press, 2004), 32.

SECTION 3
IMPACT

MODULE 9
THE FIRST RESPONSES

KEY POINTS

- Critics have accused Weber of ignoring other causal factors in the development of capitalism* and overestimating the role Protestantism* played in establishing the "spirit of capitalism."*

- Weber responded that he was not trying to provide a comprehensive explanation of the development of capitalism. He also defended the link between Protestant sects* and the "spirit of capitalism."

- Thanks to the originality of Weber's thesis, the work had a very positive reception.

Criticism

The historians H. Karl Fischer* and Felix Rachfahl* wrote detailed critiques of Max Weber's *The Protestant Ethic and the Spirit of Capitalism*, first published in journals. The German economists Lujo Brentano* and Werner Sombart* also criticized the work in their own books; Sombart, both an economist and a sociologist,* was one of Weber's coeditors at the journal that published Weber's work.

Critics called Weber's work one-sided. Some felt he did not fully explain the origins of capitalism. Others held that Weber focused too much on the role of ideas, ignoring other potential factors. Sombart argued that Jewish people had formed the vanguard of capitalism: "Now, if Puritanism* has had an economic influence, how much more so has Judaism,* seeing that among no other civilized people has religion so impregnated all national life."[1] Brentano offered a more specific criticism. He suggested that something like the "spirit of capitalism" existed among Roman Catholic* Italian merchants,

> **❝** In a way, the controversy over Weber's *Protestant Ethic* began even before the essay was first published **❞**
>
> Fritz Ringer, *Max Weber: An Intellectual Biography*

centuries before the Reformation.* Brentano argued that "the Italian merchant cities of Venice, Genoa, and Pisa were extremely capitalistic in their commercial operations and trading policies … before Protestantism appeared."[2] Weber, however, does not take notice of this trend.

Fischer questioned the relationship between religion and the "spirit of capitalism," arguing that "neither the capitalist spirit nor the ideas on duty Weber associated with it could necessarily be said to have been affected by religious beliefs or writings."[3] Fischer suggested that Weber did not consider strongly enough the argument that political and social forces might create the "spirit of capitalism."[4] Fischer felt that during the Reformation, ideas had changed to suit the changing economic circumstances.[5] In his view, this could have caused the link between Protestantism and capitalism.

Rachfahl also took issue with Weber's thesis, claiming "Weber had not provided sufficient evidence to substantiate his own thesis and thus failed to formulate the relationship between Protestantism and capitalism correctly."[6] Rachfahl suggests that capitalism in the Netherlands developed before Calvinism,* and many of the capitalists at the time were Roman Catholics. This was also the case in England before the Protestant sect of Puritanism took root. He claimed Weber provided little evidence that Puritan commercial activity had religious motivations.[7]

Responses

Weber replied to critics in a series of "anti-critical responses" that appeared in the *Archiv für Sozialwissenschaften und Sozialpolitik*,* the journal that had first published *The Protestant Ethic*.[8] He also responded in the full edition of *The Protestant Ethic* published in 1920.

Weber found Fischer's and Rachfahl's critiques irrelevant. It had never been his objective to totally explain the origins of capitalism; he had only wanted to inquire about the *link* between Protestantism and modern capitalism. Furthermore, he had never doubted that capitalism existed long before Calvinism. He stressed this more modest objective throughout the text and in the concluding pages. Weber also accepted his critics were correct that many of the factors they cited had helped to develop capitalism.[9]

In notes to the 1920 book edition of the essay, Weber addressed Brentano's argument that he had overlooked Roman Catholic entrepreneurs in the medieval and Renaissance periods. He maintained that Protestants, not their Roman Catholic predecessors, had introduced the methodical aspect of the capitalist economic ethic. This methodical element had provided the "intensity" of work required to break with "economic traditionalism."*[10]

To Sombart's claim that Jews had developed a norm of capitalist acquisition, Weber argued that the outsider or "pariah" status of Jews meant that they wielded less influence in society than the Puritans.[11] In Weber's view, Jews accepted this outsider status so they could maintain a "ritual purity": only "shady economic dealing with the outsider was acceptable."[12] The outsider status of Jews excluded them from "economic activity consistent with the continuous, systematic, and rationalized* industrial enterprise."[13]

Citing the academic discipline of philology* (the study of languages, involving literary criticism, history, and linguistics), Weber accused Fischer of failing to provide any compelling evidence for *his* arguments: "Philological findings may obviously correct my conclusions at any time. However, as the evidence stands, this certainly cannot be done by merely asserting the opposite."[14] Fischer replied that Weber should seek to discount all the other possible explanations so he could prove religion was the most important factor in determining economic behavior. Weber responded that this would be impossible and would involve him having to prove a negative.[15]

Weber took much the same approach in responding to Rachfahl's criticism.[16] He reasserted his argument that a person's religious vocation affects his or her conduct in life.[17] He also directed his critics to reread his original argument about the many causes of capitalism.[18]

Conflict and Consensus

The majority of the additions Weber made to the 1920 edition of *The Protestant Ethic* addressed the criticisms made by Sombart and Brentano. Although Weber treated their criticisms with more respect than he showed for Rachfahl's and Fischer's, he still dismissed them. In his additions to the 1920 text, Weber did not meaningfully change any essential elements of the 1905 essay; he only clarified his broader argument. This testifies to how strongly Weber felt about the arguments he made in *The Protestant Ethic.*

The Protestant Ethic stands as one of the most important and influential works of the twentieth century. So we should not be surprised that it has sparked an extraordinary amount of scholarship. Some academics still debate the validity of Weber's main thesis about the role Protestantism played in the development of modern capitalism. For example, the Italian German economist Davide Cantoni* has argued against Weber's thesis.[19] The Canadian economist Leonard Dudley* and the German economist Ulrich Blum,* on the other hand, have cited evidence supporting it.[20]

In general, scholars accept *The Protestant Ethic* as a classic and a foundational work. By now, more than a century after its original publication, only a few Weber specialists still debate the issues raised in *The Protestant Ethic.*

NOTES

1 Werner Sombart, *The Jews and Modern Capitalism* (Kitchener, ON: Batoche Books, 2001), 134.

2 Paul D. Schafer, *Revolution or Renaissance: Making the Transition from an Economic Age to a Cultural Age* (Ottawa: University of Ottawa Press, 2008), 30.

3 Stephen P. Turner, *The Cambridge Companion to Weber* (Cambridge: Cambridge University Press, 2000), 163–4.

4 Turner, *The Cambridge Companion to Weber*, 164.

5 Turner, *The Cambridge Companion to Weber*, 164.

6 Turner, *The Cambridge Companion to Weber*, 164.

7 Turner, *The Cambridge Companion to Weber*, 164.

8 *Archiv für Sozialwissenschaften und Sozialpolitik* (Archives for Social Science and Social Policy) was edited by Weber, Werner Sombart, and Edgar Jaffé, and became the leading German journal of the time.

9 Turner, *The Cambridge Companion to Weber*, 162.

10 Hartmut Lehmann and Guenther Roth, *Weber's Protestant Ethic: Origins, Evidence, Contexts* (Cambridge: Cambridge University Press, 1995), 228.

11 Lehmann and Roth, *Weber's Protestant Ethic*, 230.

12 Lehmann and Roth, *Weber's Protestant Ethic*, 230–1.

13 Lehmann and Roth, *Weber's Protestant Ethic*, 231.

14 Sam Whimster, *Understanding Weber* (New York: Routledge, 2007), 119.

15 Whimster, *Understanding Weber*, 119.

16 Whimster, *Understanding Weber*, 120.

17 Whimster, *Understanding Weber*, 120.

18 Max Weber, *The Protestant Ethic and the Spirit of Capitalism*, trans. Talcott Parsons (London: Routledge, 2005), 49.

19 Davide Cantoni, "The Economic Effects of the Protestant Reformation: Testing the Weber Hypothesis in the German Lands," *Journal of the European Economic Association* 13, no. 4 (2014): 561–98.

20 Ulrich Blum and Leonard Dudley, "Religion and Economic Growth: Was Weber Right?" *Journal of Evolutionary Economics* 11, no. 2 (2001): 207–30.

THE EVOLVING DEBATE

KEY POINTS

- *The Protestant Ethic* had a deep impact on how people thought about the development of capitalism* and modern society.

- The schools of thought that emerged from the work included the functionalist* theories of Talcott Parsons* as well as conflict theories* inspired by Marxist* thought. "Functionalism" is a theoretical approach that considers society as a whole body composed of parts that contribute different functions to sustain it.

- *The Protestant Ethic* remains a foundational text in sociology* and continues to influence current scholarship.

Uses and Problems

Readings of Max Weber's *The Protestant Ethic and the Spirit of Capitalism* have changed significantly since its publication. The original debate concentrated on whether or not its thesis, now called the "Weber thesis," was factually correct. While this debate continued, sociologists began to focus more on the theoretical implications of Weber's findings, asking how different subfields could apply them.

The sociologist Talcott Parsons translated the work into English in 1930. That translation brought the work to wider attention in the global academic community. It was then—in the 1930s and 1940s—that *The Protestant Ethic* acquired its status as a foundational work in the field of sociology. Parsons translated and interpreted the text in a way that brought it closer to the French sociologist Émile Durkheim's* functionalism[1] (an approach that seeks to identify the useful "purpose" of the different forms of social behavior that constitute a society). But

> **❝** Capitalism is identical with the pursuit of profit,
> and forever renewed profit, by means of continuous,
> rational, capitalistic enterprise. **❞**
>
> Max Weber, *The Protestant Ethic*

this interpretation also put Weber in opposition to Karl Marx,* underplaying the role of material interests and conflict in the development of capitalism.[2]

In the 1970s and 1980s, three of the most important contemporary sociological theorists—Pierre Bourdieu* in France, Anthony Giddens* in Great Britain, and Jürgen Habermas* in Germany—synthesized Marx, Weber, and Durkheim in their own theories of "practice," "structuration,"* and "communicative action,"* respectively.[3] In addition to drawing on Weber's ideas of domination and conflict, they also borrowed new ideas from *The Protestant Ethic*. They analyzed the "styles of life" developed in modern capitalism, recalling some of Weber's now-classic concepts such as the "disenchantment of the world"* (the idea that magical beliefs could not coexist with the increasingly rational nature of Western thought).

Today, most of the debates about *The Protestant Ethic* center not so much on its relevance for grand sociological theories, but on its applications in different subfields of sociology. Only scholars who specialize in interpreting Weber, including *The Protestant Ethic*, tend to go further than this. These include the British historian Peter Ghosh* and the Swedish sociologist Richard Swedberg.*

Schools of Thought

Max Weber conceived *The Protestant Ethic* as a response to the Marxist* economist Werner Sombart's* 1902 work *Der Moderne Kapitalismus*. Scholars have traditionally seen the text, at least in part, as a critique of Marxist materialist conceptions of history.* But from the late 1950s, and especially in the 1960s and 1970s, the text began to influence Marxist-inspired sociologists, whose "conflict theories" bridged Marx and Weber and served as a counterpoint to Talcott Parsons's more functionalist interpretation.

Rather than stressing consensus over values, some scholars emphasized Weber's account of conflict, interests, domination, bureaucracy,* and rationality. These included the American sociologists C. Wright Mills* and Alvin Gouldner* and the German British sociologist Ralf Dahrendorf,* among others. Mills's *White Collar: The American Middle Classes*,[4] for example, expands on Weber's arguments about the process of bureaucratization (the increasing social importance of practices of administration in things such as government and business). In *Patterns of Industrial Behavior*,[5] Alvin Gouldner (a Marxist sociologist) discusses the extent to which bureaucracy could be used to dominate individuals. Weber has also inspired a number of scholars who may be called "pure Weberians." They do not synthesize his theory with those of other major authors; instead, they focus on interpreting Weber's work from the point of view of its original context and purposes, applying his ideas to help us understand other times and places. German and British scholars remain notable in this tradition, with Reinhard Bendix* and Bryan S. Turner* among the most influential.

Various schools within subfields of sociology have also adopted *The Protestant Ethic*. For instance, in economic sociology* (inquiry into the ways in which economic behavior is embedded in society), the Swedish sociologist Richard Swedberg* argues, among other things, for assuming less rational* action and taking more seriously value-rational* and traditional, economic action ("value-rational" signifying an action performed for its inherent value, rather than to achieve a specific goal). This has been highly influential.[6]

In Current Scholarship

Scholars inspired by Weber continue to produce novel contributions, most notably in the areas of sociological theory, political science, and economic sociology. For example, the highly influential Indian anthropologist* Arjun Appadurai,* influenced by Weber's "spirit of capitalism,"* has written on the "spirit" of calculation.

Many of Weber's adherents, such as the German sociologist Wolfgang Schluchter,* have found that Weber's main contribution hinges on his understanding of Western rationalization—the process by which rational thought becomes increasingly predominant in social life. This process occurs in religion, work, accounting, politics, and law, although not always in a mutually related way. Jürgen Habermas finds that Weber's diagnosis of modern societies serves as the foundational sociological support for understanding rationally justifiable decisions. And he means this not only in terms of a philosophical ideal but also as an actual possibility. In other words, the sociological basis of Habermas's influential political theory of deliberative democracy* (a form of democracy in which decision-making is founded on discussion and reflections) owes much to Weber.[7]

Another scholar concerned with modernization and inspired by Weber is the American political scientist Ronald Inglehart.* Weber demonstrated that as countries become more capitalistic, their values shift. They move from traditional to modern materialist* values—those emphasizing economic and physical security—when their economies become more capitalistic. Inglehart takes this further. He argues that as wealthier countries continue to develop they embrace values concerned with self-expression and quality of life.[8] Taking a different approach, French sociologists Luc Boltanski* and his coauthor Ève Chiapello* note that capitalism still needs a spirit. They argue that in the modern world, most people do not seek this spirit in religion. Instead, they may find it in a class of managers and executives inspired by management ideology.[9]

In the discipline of economic sociology, Richard Swedberg has pioneered a Weber-inspired research program. He aims to provide an alternative to the focus on rational decisions and networks. By calling attention to the role of values and tradition in economic action, Swedberg has helped to redefine the subfield. Many other scholars have just made assumptions about these issues. Swedberg has also argued that Weber inspired Pierre Bourdieu's important contributions to the subfield. He believes Bordieu's work on the "disenchantment of the world" and its relevance to understanding Algerian peasants owes something to Weber's *The Protestant Ethic*.[10]

NOTES

1   Michele Dillon, *Introduction to Sociological Theory: Theorists, Concepts, and Their Applicability to the Twenty-First Century* (Chichester: John Wiley & Sons, 2009), 156.

2   Ken Morrison, *Marx, Durkheim, Weber: Formations of Modern Social Thought* (London: Sage, 2006), 295.

3   Paul Ransome, *Social Theory for Beginners* (Bristol: Policy, 2010), 291.

4   C. Wright Mills, *White Collar: The American Middle Classes* (Oxford: Oxford University Press, 2002).

5   Alvin W. Gouldner, *Patterns of Industrial Bureaucracy* (Free Press, 1964).

6   Richard Swedberg, *Max Weber and the Idea of Economic Sociology* (Princeton, NJ: Princeton University Press, 2000).

7   John P. McCormick, *Weber, Habermas and Transformations of the European State: Constitutional, Social, and Supranational Democracy* (Cambridge: Cambridge University Press, 2007), 30.

8   Ronald Inglehart, *Modernization and Postmodernization: Cultural, Economic, and Political Change in 43 Societies* (Princeton, NJ: Princeton University Press, 1997).

9   Luc Boltanski and Eve Chiapello, "The New Spirit of Capitalism," *International Journal of Politics, Culture, and Society* 18, no. 3–4 (2005): 161–88.

10 Richard Swedberg, "The Economic Sociologies of Pierre Bourdieu," *Cultural Sociology* 5, no. 1 (2011): 69.

IMPACT AND INFLUENCE TODAY

KEY POINTS

- Scholars still consider *The Protestant Ethic* a classic text and a foundational piece of work in the discipline of sociology.*

- More than a century after its publication, *The Protestant Ethic* still fuels debate about the origins of modern capitalist* society.

- While some specialists continue to debate Weber's argument, most academic attention now focuses on applying Weber's ideas to new disciplines.

Position

Max Weber's *The Protestant Ethic and the Spirit of Capitalism* made a historic argument, as the British sociologist Peter Hamilton points out.[1] Weber wrote that "the religious root of modern economic humanity is dead; today the concept of the calling* is a *caput mortuum* in the world."[2] The Latin phrase literally translated as "dead head" serves to describe a "useless remnant." Since this constitutes Weber's main thesis, one might argue that *The Protestant Ethic* retains only limited relevance today. After all, Weber examined the development of capitalism. He did not concern himself with the state of the institution in our time, a hundred years later.

Yet *The Protestant Ethic* does remain relevant today, not because of its main argument but because it sparked a more general approach to thinking about social change. The American political scientist Francis Fukuyama* argues that while economists do not take Weber's cultural theory of economic growth particularly seriously, they still address his

> **❝ The present age and its presentation of itself is dominantly Weberian. ❞**
> Alasdair MacIntyre, *After Virtue*

ideas concerning the role religion and culture play in the performance of institutions.[3] This useful insight can help explain contemporary issues such as differing attitudes toward corruption in Protestant* and Roman Catholic* countries.[4] Fukuyama also suggests that *The Protestant Ethic* has raised "profound questions about the role of religion in modern life."[5]

Furthermore, Weber's account of the rationalization* of Western society appears to have been accurate. We have seen, as he did, that "rational science based capitalism has spread across the globe, bringing material advancement to large parts of the world and welding it together in the iron cage* we now call globalization."[6] It would be an overstretch to say that the work stimulated new debates. But we can certainly use the ideas in *The Protestant Ethic* in contemporary debates about the relationship between religion and economic behavior. Fukuyama suggests that the "revival of Hinduism* among middle-class Indians … or the continuing vibrancy of religion in America, suggests that secularization* and rationalism* are hardly the inevitable handmaidens of modernization."[7] This process does not exactly accord with Weber's argument in *The Protestant Ethic*, but it does illustrate the continued relevance of Weber's investigation.

Given the amount of attention *The Protestant Ethic* has received, it becomes nearly impossible to construct a consensus view of its argument. As the sociologist Bryan S. Turner* comments, "The Protestant ethic argument has been a topic of endless and continuous evaluation."[8] However, we cannot doubt that Weber's *The Protestant Ethic* remains a classic.

Interaction

As the British sociologist Anthony Giddens* comments, *The Protestant Ethic* was "written with polemical intent … and is directed against economic determinism."* For Giddens, "It seems clear that Weber has Marxism* in mind here, or at least the cruder forms of historical analysis which were prominent."[9] Weber's account of how religious ideas can determine the economic development of a society challenged Marxist economists and political theorists of his time. In demonstrating that ideas also have important power to cause events, Weber undermines the idea that material conditions determine the economic and class structure of society. As such, only contemporary thinkers who embrace Marxism as it was when Weber wrote *The Protestant Ethic* remain significantly challenged by the work.

Nevertheless, *The Protestant Ethic* still sparks debate. Scholars continue to publish challenges to Weber's thesis. But these challenges do not emerge from a theoretical or ideological clash. Instead, their writers wish to demonstrate whether or not the "Weber thesis," one of the most controversial arguments of the twentieth century, holds true. For example, Davide Cantoni* has argued against Weber's thesis,[10] while Leonard Dudley* and Ulrich Blum,* have argued for it.[11]

The Continuing Debate

Today, most of the debates about *The Protestant Ethic* focus less on its relevance to grand sociological theories, than on applying it to different subfields of sociology. Only a select group of Weber specialists still debate its original content or meaning.[12] The majority of scholars referring to it today use the work as a source of ideas for new research in related topics.

Nonetheless, some discussion of its content continues. Perhaps the most notable topic focuses on how Weber's thesis relates to the development of Western rationalization* and capitalism.[13] Contemporary scholars of comparative politics and political cultures such as Ronald Inglehart* and Anglo American political sociologist Pippa Norris* have written influential evaluations of Weber's argument that societies become more secular* as they become more rationalized.[14]

The discipline of sociology constantly revisits the concerns and approaches of its founders, and Weber continues to be one of the most influential sociologists. A new English translation of the 1920 edition of *The Protestant Ethic* appeared in 2001. This new edition standardized Weber's terminology and restored his original italicization, bringing out the nuance and subtlety of Weber's arguments.[15] The *Journal of Classical Sociology* frequently publishes material on Weber. So does the journal *Max Weber Studies*, which remains exclusively dedicated to debating Weber's work. These publications often address key topics around *The Protestant Ethic*.

NOTES

1   Peter Hamilton, ed., *Max Weber, Critical Assessments*, vol. 1. (London: Routledge, 1991), 308.

2   Hamilton, *Max Weber, Critical Assessments*, 308.

3   Francis Fukuyama, "The Calvinist Manifesto," *The New York Times*, March 13, 2005, accessed October 18, 2015, http://www.nytimes.com/2005/03/13/books/review/the-calvinist-manifesto.html.

4   Fukuyama, "The Calvinist Manifesto."

5   Fukuyama, "The Calvinist Manifesto."

6   Fukuyama, "The Calvinist Manifesto."

7   Fukuyama, "The Calvinist Manifesto."

8   Bryan S. Turner, *Max Weber: From History to Modernity* (New York: Routledge, 2002), 25.

9   Max Weber, *The Protestant Ethic and the Spirit of Capitalism: and other writings* (London and New York: Routledge, 2005), XVIII.

10 Davide Cantoni, "The Economic Effects of the Protestant Reformation: Testing the Weber Hypothesis in the German Lands," *Journal of the European Economic Association* 13, no. 4 (2014): 561–98.

11 Ulrich Blum and Leonard Dudley, "Religion and Economic Growth: Was Weber Right?" *Journal of Evolutionary Economics* 11, no. 2 (2001): 207–30.

12 Richard Swedberg, *Max Weber and the Idea of Economic Sociology* (Princeton, NJ: Princeton University Press, 2000); Peter Ghosh, *Max Weber and 'The Protestant Ethic': Twin Histories* (Oxford: Oxford University Press, 2014).

13 Nicholas Gane, *Max Weber and Postmodern Theory: Rationalization versus Re-enchantment* (Basingstoke: Palgrave, 2002).

14 Pippa Norris and Ronald Inglehart, *Sacred and Secular: Religion and Politics Worldwide* (Cambridge: Cambridge University Press, 2011).

15 Max Weber, *The Protestant Ethic and the Spirit of Capitalism: With Other Writings on the Rise of the West*, trans. Stephen Kalberg, 4th ed. (New York: Oxford University Press, 2009).

WHERE NEXT?

KEY POINTS

- *The Protestant Ethic* is likely to remain an important piece of work for many years to come.

- As capitalism* continues to evolve, the arguments in *The Protestant Ethic* concerning the development of Western capitalism and the process of rationalization* will remain relevant.

- *The Protestant Ethic* played a seminal role in establishing the discipline of sociology.*

Potential

Scholars will likely consider Max Weber's *The Protestant Ethic and the Spirit of Capitalism* a classic for a long time to come. Sociologists have been drawing on it for over a hundred years now, and this seems unlikely to change.[1] Weber remains an important figure in the discipline—and *The Protestant Ethic* is one reason why. Scholars in the subfield of general social theory have long discussed Weber. Their debate remains strong, even if their discipline has been slower to grow than other fields. But scholars in a number of growing subfields, such as economic sociology* (the study of the ways in which economics are embedded in social behavior) and cultural sociology* (the study of social structures and symbols as they are understood to form culture) have also taken to citing *The Protestant Ethic* in their work.

Many contemporary sociologists find themselves addressing problems similar to those Weber discussed a century ago. And many of the responses the early sociologists offered remain relevant today. This continuing relevance distinguishes sociology from other social

> 66 Sociology ... is a science concerning itself with the interpretive understanding of social action and thereby with a causal explanation of its course and consequences. 99
>
> Max Weber, *Economy and Society*

sciences, and makes the founding figures of the discipline particularly important. In other words, sociologists do not necessarily find *The Protestant Ethic* important as an accurate piece of empirical* scholarship. Instead, they remain attracted by its creative potential: the questions it poses and the hypotheses it allows scholars to raise. Today Weber's essay typically serves as a catalyst for related projects. It can spark debate about things like the role of culture and values in the development of the economy. It can be used to draw cross-cultural comparisons between societies. And it can aid discussions around the development of modernity and rationality.

Future Directions

As a foundational work in the discipline of sociology, *The Protestant Ethic* has given rise to an incalculable amount of scholarship. More than a century after its publication, scholars have already developed every well-defined position possible. Weber felt that history had no "iron laws,"[2] seeing the "task of social theory" to facilitate "the search for historical truths."[3] Weber rejected the Marxist* idea that academic inquiry should change society.[4] So Weberian scholars are not charged to search for any particular truth. Rather, they look to discover the truth through fair and reasonable inquiry. If Weber created followers, he wanted them to be scholars empowered to pursue their own lines of inquiry. This makes it difficult to identify any scholars in particular as Weber's heirs.

Furthermore, generations of scholars have cast considerable doubt on just about all of Weber's substantive arguments. Yes, influential thinkers such as American political scientist Francis Fukuyama* have argued for the continued importance of Weber's general claims about the influence of religion and culture on economic behavior.[5] But the British sociologist Anthony Giddens* suggests that we may question the detail of almost all of Weber's arguments: "I don't think Weber's view of methodological individualism has really stood up to the test of time … And his theory of bureaucracy* turns out to be quite time bound … And of course it is not proven that Protestantism* or Puritanism* were at the origins of modern capitalism, as Weber claimed."[6]

With question marks attached to Weber's main claims, few scholars remain willing to move these ideas forward.

Summary

In *The Protestant Ethic*, Max Weber claimed that the methodical conduct of life in search of profit served as an important force in the development of modern capitalism. And he believed that Protestant theology* inspired that profit-seeking motive. This argument, which has attracted much attention since its publication, has come to be known as the "Weber thesis." A relatively brief text, *The Protestant Ethic* addressed important problems contemporary with the birth of sociology as a discipline. Weber's followers in various schools would canonize these problems as fundamental sociological concerns and avenues of inquiry. For instance, we can trace scholarly interest in the origins and future of modern capitalism and Western rationalism* to Weber, as well as interest in the causal force of beliefs, values, tradition, and nonmaterial interests.

Weber claimed that religious ideas could cause economic change. This set him apart from early strongly "materialist"* interpretations of Marxist philosophy. For a while, scholars saw this as the core of Weber's originality. But today many scholars seek to synthesize Weber and Karl Marx,* interpreting Marx as less materialist and Weber as less focused on the role of ideas. In addition, the text contains a number of ambiguities, particularly regarding key concepts such as "elective affinities."* Partly this may be due to the 15-year period between its initial publication as an essay and its release in book form, with some key additions by Weber. In any event, Weber left room for multiple interpretations and over the years they have sparked much debate.

Ideas in *The Protestant Ethic* have sparked the creation of new hypotheses. Even some of its less central concepts—the "disenchantment of the world"* or the "iron cage,"* for example—have become classic sociological concepts in their own right. And scholars have come to regard many of Weber's other works as classics too. For decades, sociologists have almost unanimously considered him a founder of the discipline, alongside Karl Marx and Émile Durkheim.*

As they value other great works by the founders of sociology, scholars will continue to value *The Protestant Ethic* for a long time. Many contemporary sociological research programs and theories have grown from the problems it raises and responses great thinkers have had to them. Indeed, these responses have largely defined the discipline of sociology. Anyone interested in sociology will find inspiration in Weber's work in general and *The Protestant Ethic* in particular.

NOTES

1   Kieran Allen, *Max Weber: A Critical Introduction* (Pluto Press, 2004), 32.

2   Guenther Roth and Wolfgang Schluchter, *Max Weber's Vision of History: Ethics and Methods* (Berkeley, CA: University of California Press, 1984), 201.

3   Ken Morrison, *Marx, Durkheim, Weber: Formations of Modern Social Thought* (London: Sage, 2006), 276.

4   Morrison, *Marx, Durkheim, Weber*, 276.

5   Francis Fukuyama, "The Calvinist Manifesto," *The New York Times*, March 13, 2005, accessed October 18, 2015, http://www.nytimes. com/2005/03/13/books/review/the-calvinist-manifesto.html.

6   Anthony Giddens and Christopher Pierson, *Conversations with Anthony Giddens: Making Sense of Modernity* (Stanford, CA: Stanford University Press, 1998), 60–1.

GLOSSARY

GLOSSARY OF TERMS

Ancient Rome: a civilization that began in the eighth century B.C.E. One of the biggest and most significant empires in the ancient world, it lasted until the fifth century C.E.

Anthropology: the study of humankind. This can often involve comparative studies of different cultures and investigating how different social structures have evolved.

Archiv für Sozialwissenschaften und Sozialpolitik **(Archive for Social Science and Social Policy):** a journal edited by Weber, Werner Sombart, and Edgar Jaffé. It was the leading German academic journal of the time.

Asceticism: Weber used the term to refer to the self-denial of pleasure. He suggested that in modern capitalism self-control and self-denial became a form of social action that created a disciplined approach to work. This asceticism had religious roots. But Weber claimed that by the nineteenth century, asceticism had become part of everyday life.

Baptists: a group within the Protestant branch of philosophy who believe that baptisms should only be performed on believers. So they oppose the common practice of baptizing infants. They also believe that baptism must involve the full immersion of the person being baptized under water.

Buddhism: a movement concerned with the spiritual development of the individual. Buddhists do not believe in a creator or personal God, but do believe that to reach nirvana—a transcendent state— people must follow the path of the Buddha. Today there are nearly 400 million Buddhists worldwide.

Bureaucracy: Weber used the term to refer to a particular type of administrative structure, associated with the process of rationalization. For example, it involved a hierarchical structure with members being selected on the basis of merit rather than social ties.

Calling: having a "calling" implied that one's work was a God-given task. The sixteenth-century German theologian Martin Luther advanced this notion.

Calvinism: A branch of Protestantism associated with the French cleric and reformer John Calvin. Calvinism emphasizes the rule of God over all things. In its earliest form, it taught predestination (the concept that some people were destined for heaven and others were not, despite the good works they might do during their lifetimes).

Capitalism: in Weber's definition, this is an economic and social system that existed in most civilizations when economic enterprise began to calculate expected profit both before an enterprise had been undertaken and again at the end of the project. The differences would then be compared for all possible transactions. "Modern capitalism" or "Western capitalism" is a more specific organization of the economy that emerged in Western Europe and the United States. In modern capitalism, free labor is organized in a rational—calculated—manner, and the "spirit of capitalism" guides society in the systematic pursuit of profit. A more general understanding of capitalism is a system where private individuals own capital and the means of production are not collectively owned.

Common law: a law that, instead of being made by statute, is developed by judges. The decisions made by judges in individual cases serve as precedents in the law, meaning past decisions bind the future decisions of judges.

Communicative action: a term the German philosopher Jürgen Habermas used to describe action based on deliberation and argument undertaken by groups of individuals.

Confucianism: a way of life based on the teachings of Confucius, a Chinese philosopher whose life spanned the fifth and sixth centuries B.C.E.

Cultural sociology: the study of the social behavior and symbols as they are understood to constitute "culture."

Culturalism: a concept that emphasizes the importance of culture in determining social behavior.

Deliberative democracy: a form of democracy in which public deliberation is the basis of legitimate decision-making.

Diaspora: a dispersed group of people. It most often describes people forced to leave their homeland, but can be used for voluntary migration.

Disenchantment of the world: a phrase used by Weber to indicate the process by which magic ceases to have a role in mediating humans' relation to the world. Protestantism (especially Calvinism) played a role in this disenchantment by disavowing the Roman Catholic belief that the Church could help save people's souls.

Economic determinism: the idea that economic relationships are fundamental to explaining social phenomena. This idea remains most associated with the work of Karl Marx.

Economic sociology: the study of the social causes of economic institutions and behaviors. The label was first used in the late nineteenth century. *The Protestant Ethic* is considered to be one of the most important works in economic sociology.

Economic traditionalism: a culture or economic ethic that views work as a necessary evil, less valuable than leisure, which should be performed only as required to satisfy "traditional needs."

Elective affinity/inner affinity: a somewhat ambiguous term that recurs in Weber's work, this has been the subject of some debate. It denotes a relationship between two phenomena connected by a common feature or a historical link, but which cannot be clearly demonstrated to have a causal link. Thus, Protestant beliefs did not "cause" the spirit of capitalism, but they are highly compatible with it.

Empirical: a term used to describe knowledge derived from the process of observation and experiment. We gather empirical knowledge by means of the senses.

Epistemology: a branch of philosophy concerned with the study of knowledge.

Eurocentrism: viewing the world from a purely European perspective. It generally involves a belief that European culture is superior to other cultures.

Eurozone: the collective term for all of the countries that use the euro as their currency. The eurozone includes countries such as Germany, France, and Spain.

Feudalism: a medieval social system in which status and authority were closely bound up with land ownership and labor.

Functionalism: a theoretical approach that, inspired by biology, looks at society as a whole body composed of parts that contribute different functions to sustain it. The concept has its roots in the French philosopher Auguste Comte and the British philosopher Herbert Spencer. Émile Durkheim became the first sociologist to employ functionalist thought. Weber's translator Talcott Parsons and his follower American sociologist Robert K. Merton further elaborated the theory, making it the dominant perspective in the 1940s and 1950s.

Habilitation thesis or *Habilitationsschrift*: a professorial thesis required for habilitation, the highest academic degree—beyond even a PhD—in some European and Asian countries.

Heidelberg University: founded in 1386, it is the oldest university in Germany. It has a historic reputation for independent thought and democratic values.

Hinduism: a religion with over 900 million followers worldwide, mainly in India and Nepal. It is one of the world's oldest religions, dating back thousands of years.

Historical materialism: Karl Marx's "materialist conception of history" explains historical change in ideas, or the ideological superstructure, as a consequence rather than the cause of changes in the economic infrastructure.

Humanities: academic disciplines that study human culture. They include history, literature, and philosophy.

Idealism: the term used to describe the philosophical viewpoint that reality is a mental phenomenon. As such, human behavior has to be understood through interpretation of social values and cannot be reduced to material interests.

Industrial Revolution: the term used to describe the period of economic transformation via the adoption of new manufacturing processes that started in the United Kingdom in the mid-eighteenth century and then spread to Western Europe over the next one hundred years.

Interpretative sociology or sociology of understanding (*verstehen*): a sociological approach developed notably by Weber and Georg Simmel, it focused not on describing facts, but on explaining the causes and consequences of actions by understanding their subjective *meaning*.

Iron cage: Weber concluded, metaphorically, that humans do not control their concern for material goods any more. The desire has turned into a "steel-hard casing." The first English translator of *The Protestant Ethic*, Talcott Parsons, rendered the term as "iron cage." His metaphor has become a classic concept associated with this work.

Judaism: one of the oldest world religions, dating back 3500 years. Jews believe that as God's chosen people they should endeavor to live a holy and ethical life.

Lutheranism: the name given to a branch of Protestantism that follows the theology of Martin Luther. One of the main tenets of Lutheranism is that scripture is the final authority on all religious matters.

Marxism: a socioeconomic theory developed by Karl Marx. Marxism holds that class conflict is the driving force of history and that economic interests determine the material and ideological structure of society.

Methodism: a religious movement begun in the eighteenth century that originally sought to reform the Church of England. Just before the end of the eighteenth century, however, it established itself as an autonomous Church.

Middle Ages: a period of European history lasting from the fifth century to the fifteenth. It is considered the middle period of history, coming after the early period of antiquity and before the modern period.

Neo-Kantianism: a branch of philosophy deeply influenced by the work of eighteenth-century German philosopher Immanuel Kant. It was Germany's leading philosophical movement between the 1870s and World War I.

Pietism: a reform movement among Lutherans in the seventeenth century. It emphasized the importance of personal faith above all else.

Philology: the study of language and languages, involving a combination of literary criticism, history, and linguistics.

Positivism: a branch of the philosophy of science and epistemology founded by the nineteenth-century French philosopher Auguste Comte, who coined the term "sociology." Positivism claims that the only valid knowledge is that which can be expressed as laws verified by experience. Positivism became most influential through the work of one of the fathers of sociology, Émile Durkheim.

Predestination: the belief that the fate of the individual's soul has been decided by God and will arrive regardless of the individual's behavior. The term is also used to refer to other events ordained by God.

Premodern: the period up until the fifteenth century. Scholars usually characterize it as a period in which tradition and religion dominated social life.

Progressive Christianity: a theological movement common to all Christian denominations, it links Christianity with progressive concerns such as social justice.

Protestantism: a form of Christianity. It emerged following the Reformation and the split with Roman Catholicism.

Prussia: a historic state that existed between 1525 and 1947 in what is now northern Germany and parts of Poland.

Puritanism: For Weber, Puritanism involved self-denial of pleasure and a distancing of oneself from the world. Protestant sects such as Calvinism encouraged this type of behavior. Puritanism aimed to remove the Roman Catholic influence on Protestant worship.

Quakers: the term commonly used for members of the religious group the Society of Friends. The movement, which began in the mid-seventeenth century, stresses the importance of living according to one's direct knowledge of God's will.

Rational accounting: the term Weber uses to describe the process of estimating profit and loss before transactions are undertaken, as well as after they have taken place.

Rational(ism): Weber used this term to refer to both types of societies and types of behavior. A rational society used rational legal standards, rational accounting methods and exhibited a general mastery of nature. Rational behaviors are actions precisely calculated to achieve a given end.

Rationalization: a key concept in Weber's account of history and how societies developed. Rationalization involved social life being determined to a greater and greater degree by calculation and rational behavior.

Reformation: a movement begun in the sixteenth century to reform the Roman Catholic Church. The Protestant denominations emerged in Western Europe as a result of the Reformation. The process was led notably by theologians Martin Luther in Germany and John Calvin in France, among others.

Roman Catholicism: a tradition within the Christian Church that dates back 2000 years. It is the largest of all the Christian religious traditions with over 1.2 billion followers worldwide.

Sects: religious groups. Unlike Churches, they admit only members who fulfill certain criteria. Membership implies submitting to the group's monitoring of one's good character.

Secular: refers to something separate from religious institutions and religious beliefs. For example, secular education is not directed by religious teaching or undertaken by religious institutions.

Sociology: the academic study of the way humans behave. This can involve behavior from the individual level to the whole of society. Sociology seeks to explain this behavior by examining the origins of social human behavior, the way it is organized, and how humans behave under different systems of rules.

Sociology of organizations: the study of formal and informal institutions. It focuses on how these institutions are structured and the way they determine individuals' behavior.

"Spirit of capitalism": Weber used this phrase to refer to the systematic organization of life around money, profit, work, competition, and material success as ends in themselves. The "spirit of capitalism," according to Weber, came about following Calvin's teachings on salvation. Calvin emphasized personal self-control, which then extended to self-control in one's economic behavior.

Structuration theory: developed by the sociologist Anthony Giddens. It holds that while social life is more than the sum of individual acts, it is not just determined by social forces. Because people interact with social structures, structures such as traditions can be changed over time.

Taoism: a Chinese tradition of philosophy and religious belief. Taoism is concerned with following the Tao, translated as "the way." The substance of the Tao is difficult to define, but it is best understood as the creative principle of the universe.

Theology: a term that can be used to refer to the study of religious ideas. It can also be used as a collective term for specific religious ideas and concepts collectively, e.g., Protestant theology.

Unitarianism: a theology characterized by understanding God as one being—against the more common Christian interpretation of God as a Trinity, simultaneously Father, Son, and Holy Spirit.

University of Freiburg: founded in 1457, it is the fifth-oldest university in Germany, with a long tradition of education in the social and natural sciences.

Utilitarianism: a normative ethical theory that claims that a morally right act is one that maximizes utility. Utility is usually understood in terms of happiness, meaning a moral action will maximize pleasure and minimize pain.

Verein für Socialpolitik (**Social Policy Association**): an influential society of German economists founded in 1873. Its members included Max Weber and Werner Sombart.

Vocation: an ethic of work marked by the feeling of a "calling" or God-given task. While Weber searched for this type of belief among many religions, he found it only in Protestantism.

World War I: a global conflict centered in Europe between 1914 and 1918. The war involved countries such as France, Britain, Russia, and the United States on one side and Germany, Austria-Hungary, and the Ottoman Empire on the other.

PEOPLE MENTIONED IN THE TEXT

Arjun Appadurai (b. 1949) is an Indian anthropologist based in the United States, one of the most influential contemporary authors in the study of modernity and globalization. His most famous book, *Modernity at Large: Cultural Dimensions of Globalization* (1996), contains various references to Weber.

Sascha O. Becker (b. 1973) is a German economist currently working at the University of Warwick. His research interests include economic history and labor economics.

Reinhard Bendix (1916–91) was a German sociologist who immigrated to the United States. His most influential work was *Max Weber: An Intellectual Portrait* (1960).

James Blaut (1927–2000), a professor of anthropology and geography at the University of Illinois, was one of the foremost critics of Eurocentrism.

Ulrich Blum (b. 1953) is a German economist at Martin Luther University of Halle-Wittenberg in Germany. His research interests include institutional economics and industrial economics.

Luc Boltanski (b. 1940) is a leading figure in the French school of "pragmatic sociology." His most famous work is *The New Spirit of Capitalism* (1999), coauthored with Ève Chiapello.

Pierre Bourdieu (1930–2002) was an important French sociologist and philosopher, most famous for his books *Distinction: A Social Critique of the Judgment of Taste* (1984) and *Outline of a Theory of Practice* (1977).

Both of these works have been translated into English by Richard Nice.

Lujo Brentano (1844–1931) was a German economist and contemporary of Weber. Weber engages most notably with his book *The Beginnings of Modern Capitalism* (1916).

John Calvin (1509–64) was a French theologian and influential figure during the Protestant Reformation. He became associated with a branch of Protestantism called Calvinism, which held that all individuals are predestined by God to achieve either salvation or damnation.

Davide Cantoni (b. 1981) is an Italian German economist at the Ludwig Maximilian University of Munich. His research interests include economic history and political economy.

Ève Chiapello (b. 1965) is a French professor of management, best known for coauthoring *The New Spirit of Capitalism* (1999).

Ralf Dahrendorf (1929–2009) was a German British sociologist and politician, most influential for his development of conflict theory in *Class and Class Conflict in Industrial Society* (1957).

Wilhelm Dilthey (1833–1911) was a German philosopher best known for his *Introduction to the Human Sciences: An Attempt to Lay a Foundation for the Study of Society and History* (1923).

Leonard Dudley (b. 1943) is a Canadian economist working at the University of Montreal. His research interests include the effect of information technology on economic growth and political institutions.

Émile Durkheim (1858–1917) was a French sociologist most famous for his books *The Elementary Forms of Religious Life* (1912), *Suicide* (1897), and *The Division of Labour in Society* (1893).

H. Karl Fischer has not been clearly identified. Many Karl Fischers worked in German academia in Weber's day and he has no famous works other than the debate with Weber. It seems most likely that he was a scholar of German history born in 1840.

Benjamin Franklin (1706–90) was one of the Founding Fathers of the United States. Aside from being a politician he was a scientist, a printer, a diplomat, an inventor, and an author.

Francis Fukuyama (b. 1952) is an American political scientist and theorist. His best-known work is *The End of History and the Last Man* (1992) in which he controversially argued that following the fall of the Soviet Union, liberal capitalism had become the final form of human government.

Peter Ghosh is a British historian at the University of Oxford. His research interests include the interface between English politics and political ideas in the nineteenth century, and Max Weber.

Anthony Giddens (b. 1938) is an influential British sociologist best known for his *The Constitution of Society: Outline of the Theory of Structuration* (1984). Scholars consider Giddens to be one of the most important modern sociologists—if not *the* most important. He is the fifth most-referenced author in the humanities.

Eberhard Gothein (1853–1923) was a historian of culture and economics and a strong supporter of the foundation of the German Society for Sociology. He is most famous for his *Economic History of the Black Forest* (1892).

Alvin W. Gouldner (1920–80) was an important Marxist sociologist in the United States, most famous for his books *The Coming Crisis of Western Sociology* (1970) and *Patterns of Industrial Bureaucracy* (1954). The latter work applies Weberian concepts to the study of industrial relations.

Jürgen Habermas (b. 1929) is an influential German sociologist and philosopher, most famous for his *Theory of Communicative Action* (1981), which contains a full section on *The Protestant Ethic*.

Ronald Inglehart (b. 1934) is an influential political scientist in the United States, most famous for his book *Modernization and Postmodernization: Cultural, Economic, and Political Change in 43 Societies* (1997).

Edgar Jaffé (1861–1921) was a student of Max Weber and Werner Sombart, and an editor of the *Archive for the Social Sciences and Social Policy*. Jaffé's scholarly work focused on the workings of the English economy.

Georg Jellinek (1851–1911) was an Austrian lawyer and philosopher of law, best known for *The Declaration of the Rights of Man and Citizens* (1895), which inspired him to study the social consequences of Puritanism.

Martin Luther (1483–1546) was a German theologian whose writings helped inspire the Protestant Reformation. In 1534, he published a complete translation of the Bible in German, believing that people should be able to read it in their own language. Lutheranism is a branch of Protestantism that identifies with the theology of Martin Luther.

Karl Marx (1818–83) was a German philosopher, journalist, economist, sociologist, and revolutionary, most famous for writing *The Communist Manifesto* (1848)—with Friedrich Engels—and *Das Kapital* (1867–94).

Charles Wright Mills (1916–62), one of the most influential mid-twentieth-century sociologists in the United States, was most famous for writing *The Power Elite* (1956) and *The Sociological Imagination* (1959). With the sociologist Hans H. Gerth he cotranslated selections of Weber's writing, published as *From Max Weber* (1948). This book played a key role in making Weber available to the English-speaking world.

Pippa Norris (b. 1953) is a political scientist based at Harvard University. Her research interests include gender politics and the barriers women face in politics, as well as the relevance and roots of political culture.

Talcott Parsons (1902–79) was one of the most influential sociologists in the United States and parts of Europe in the mid-twentieth century. He received his PhD from Heidelberg, where he studied with Max Weber's friend the philosopher Karl Jaspers, his brother Alfred Weber, and the classical sociologist Karl Mannheim. Other than his 1930 translation of *The Protestant Ethic*, his most famous work is *The Social System* (1951).

Sir William Petty (1623–87) was a British political economist who wrote about the role of the state in the economy. In addition to his economic work he was a qualified doctor, a professor of music, and a member of the British Parliament.

Felix Rachfahl (1867–1925) was a historian of German and Dutch history, mostly known for his discussion with Weber about *The Protestant Ethic and the Spirit of Capitalism*.

Heinrich Rickert (1863–1936) was a leading figure of the Baden school of neo-Kantian philosophy and a friend of Weber. He is best known for writing *The Limits of Concept Formation in Natural Science: A Logical Introduction to the Historical Sciences* (1896 and 1902).

Wolfgang Schluchter (b. 1938) is a leading figure among German Weberian sociologists and editor of Max Weber's complete works in German. He is best known for his book *The Rise of Western Rationalism: Max Weber's Developmental History* (1979).

Georg Simmel (1858–1918), a philosopher and sociologist, ranks among the most important classical sociologists. With Weber, he cofounded the German Society for Sociology. His most influential works are *The Metropolis and Mental Life* (1903) and *The Philosophy of Money* (1907).

Werner Sombart (1863–1941) was a Marxist economist and sociologist. He is famous in English-language sociology not only for his controversy with Weber on modern capitalism, but also for his book *Why Is There No Socialism in the United States?* (1906). This seminal work deals with American exceptionalism—the idea that the United States believes it differs from other industrialized countries, especially in its politics.

Richard Swedberg (b. 1948) is a Swedish sociologist working in the United States. One of his best-known works is *Max Weber and the Idea of Economic Sociology* (2000).

Alexis de Tocqueville (1805–59) was a French political theorist and historian. He is best known for his two-volume study of American society *Democracy in America* (1835 and 1840).

Ernst Troeltsch (1865–1923) was a theologian, best known for his book *The Social Teaching of the Christian Churches* (1911), which Weber described as a confirmation and supplement to his essay.

Bryan S. Turner (b. 1945) is a British Australian sociologist most famous for writing *The Body and Society: Explorations in Social Theory* (1984). He is also coauthor of *Max Weber on Economy and Society* and the editor of the *Journal of Classical Sociology*, which frequently publishes new work about Weber.

Marianne Weber (1870–1954) a sociologist and women's rights activist who married Max Weber. She posthumously published her husband's unpublished work, including his magnum opus *Economy and Society*, and she wrote the authoritative *Max Weber: A Biography* (1926).

Wilhelm Windelband (1848–1915), another leading figure of the Badenschool of neo-Kantian philosophy, was most famous for his 1893 work *A History of Philosophy*.

Ludger Woessmann is a German economist working at the University of Munich. His research interests included the determinants of long-run prosperity and the determinants of student achievement.

WORKS CITED

WORKS CITED

Allen, Kieran. *Max Weber: A Critical Introduction*. London: Pluto Press, 2004.

Arnot, Chris. "Protestant v Catholic: Which Countries Are More Successful?" *Guardian*, October 31, 2011. Accessed September 5, 2015. http://www. theguardian.com/education/2011/oct/31/economics-religion-research.

Baehr, Peter. "The 'Iron Cage' and the 'Shell as Hard as Steel': Parsons, Weber, and the Stahlhartes Gehäuse Metaphor in the Protestant Ethic and the Spirit of Capitalism." *History and Theory* 40, no. 2 (2001): 153–69.

Barker, James R. "Tightening the Iron Cage: Concertive Control in Self-Managing Teams." *Administrative Science Quarterly* 38, no. 3 (1993): 408–37.

Becker, Sascha O., and Ludger Wohmann. "Was Weber Wrong? A Human Capital Theory of Protestant Economic History." Program on Education Policy and Governance, Harvard University (2007).

Bell, Daniel. "The Protestant Ethic." *World Policy Journal* 13, no. 3 (1996): 35–9.

Blaut, J. M. *Eight Eurocentric Historians*. New York: Guilford Press, 2000.

Blum, Ulrich, and Leonard Dudley. "Religion and Economic Growth: Was Weber Right?" *Journal of Evolutionary Economics* 11, no. 2 (2001): 207–30.

Boltanski, Luc, and Eve Chiapello. "The New Spirit of Capitalism." *International Journal of Politics, Culture, and Society* 18, no. 3–4 (2005): 161–88.

Cantoni, Davide. "The Economic Effects of the Protestant Reformation: Testing the Weber Hypothesis in the German Lands." *Journal of the European Economic Association* 13, no. 4 (2014): 561–98.

Dillon, Michele. *Introduction to Sociological Theory: Theorists, Concepts, and Their Applicability to the Twenty-First Century*. Chichester: John Wiley & Sons, 2009.

Edles, Laura Desfor, and Scott Appelrouth. *Sociological Theory in the Classical Era: Text and Readings*. Third edition. Thousand Oaks, CA: Sage, 2014.

Fukuyama, Francis. "The Calvinist Manifesto." *The New York Times*, March 13, 2005. Accessed October 18, 2015. http://www.nytimes.com/2005/03/13/ books/review/the-calvinist-manifesto.html.

Gane, Nicholas. *Max Weber and Postmodern Theory: Rationalization versus Re-enchantment*. Basingstoke: Palgrave, 2002.

Ghosh, Peter. *Max Weber and 'The Protestant Ethic': Twin Histories*. Oxford: Oxford University Press, 2014.

Giddens, Anthony, and Christopher Pierson. *Conversations with Anthony Giddens: Making Sense of Modernity*. Stanford, CA: Stanford University Press, 1998.

Gouldner, Alvin W. *Patterns of Industrial Bureaucracy*. Glencoe, IL: Free Press, 1954.

Hamilton, Peter, ed. *Max Weber, Critical Assessments*. Vol. 1. London: Routledge, 1991.

Harrison, Lawrence E., and Samuel P. Huntington. *Culture Matters: How Values Shape Human Progress*. New York: Basic Books, 2000.

Inglehart, Ronald. *Modernization and Postmodernization: Cultural, Economic, and Political Change in 43 Societies*. Princeton, NJ: Princeton University Press, 1997.

Lehmann, Hartmut, and Guenther Roth. *Weber's Protestant Ethic: Origins, Evidence, Contexts*. Cambridge: Cambridge University Press, 1995.

MacIntyre, Alasdair (1984) *After Virtue: A Study in Moral Theory*. Second edition. Notre Dame, IN: University of Notre Dame Press.

McCormick, John P. *Weber, Habermas and Transformations of the European State: Constitutional, Social, and Supranational Democracy*. Cambridge: Cambridge University Press, 2007.

Mills, C. Wright. *White Collar: The American Middle Classes*. Oxford: Oxford University Press, 2002.

Morrison, Ken. *Marx, Durkheim, Weber: Formations of Modern Social Thought*. London: Sage, 2006.

Nee, Victor and Richard Swedburg, *On Capitalism*. Stanford, CA: Stanford University Press, 2007.

Norris, Pippa, and Ronald Inglehart. *Sacred and Secular: Religion and Politics Worldwide*. Cambridge: Cambridge University Press, 2011.

Ransome, Paul. *Social Theory for Beginners*. Bristol: Policy, 2010.

Ringer, Fritz. *Max Weber: An Intellectual Biography*. Chicago: University of Chicago Press, 2010.

Roth, Guenther and Wolfgang Schluchter. *Max Weber's Vision of History: Ethics and Methods.* Berkeley, CA: University of California Press (1984).

Schafer, D. Paul. *Revolution or Renaissance: Making the Transition from an Economic Age to a Cultural Age*. Ottawa: University of Ottawa Press, 2008.

Sombart, Werner. *Der moderne Kapitalismus: Bd. Die Genesis des Kapitalismus*. Vol. 1. Leipzig: Duncker & Humblot, 1902.

The Jews and Modern Capitalism. Kitchener, ON: Batoche Books, 2001.

Swedberg, Richard. "The Economic Sociologies of Pierre Bourdieu." *Cultural Sociology* 5, no. 1 (2011): 67–82.

Max Weber and the Idea of Economic Sociology. Princeton, NJ: Princeton University Press, 2000.

Tenbruck, Friedrich H. "The Problem of Thematic Unity in the Works of Max Weber." *British Journal of Sociology* 31, no. 3 (1980): 316–51.

Turner, Bryan S. *Max Weber: From History to Modernity*. New York: Routledge, 2002.

Turner, Stephen P. *The Cambridge Companion to Weber*. Cambridge: Cambridge University Press, 2000.

Weber, Marianne. *Max Weber: A Biography*. Translated and edited by Harry Zohn. New Brunswick, NJ: Transaction Publishers, 1988.

Weber, Max. *Economy and Society: An Outline of Interpretive Sociology*. Edited by Guenther Roth and Claus Wittich. Berkeley, CA: University of California Press, 1978.

 The Protestant Ethic and the Spirit of Capitalism. Translated by Talcott Parsons. London: Routledge, 2005.

The Protestant Ethic and the "Spirit" of Capitalism: And Other Writings. Translated by Peter Baehr and Gordon C. Wells. New York: Penguin, 2002.

The Protestant Ethic and the Spirit of Capitalism: With Other Writings on the Rise of the West. Translated by Stephen Kalberg. Fourth edition. New York: Oxford University Press, 2009.

"The Protestant Sects and the Spirit of Capitalism." In *The Protestant Ethic and the "Spirit" of Capitalism: And Other Writings*. Translated by Peter Baehr and Gordon C. Wells. New York: Penguin, 2002.

The Religion of China: Confucianism and Taoism. Translated by Hans H. Gerth. New York: Free Press, 1951.

"Science as a Vocation." *Daedalus* 87, no. 1 (1958): 111–34.

Whimster, Sam. *Understanding Weber*. New York: Routledge, 2007.

THE MACAT LIBRARY
BY DISCIPLINE

The Macat Library By Discipline

AFRICANA STUDIES

Chinua Achebe's *An Image of Africa: Racism in Conrad's Heart of Darkness*
W. E. B. Du Bois's *The Souls of Black Folk*
Zora Neale Huston's *Characteristics of Negro Expression*
Martin Luther King Jr's *Why We Can't Wait*
Toni Morrison's *Playing in the Dark: Whiteness in the American Literary Imagination*

ANTHROPOLOGY

Arjun Appadurai's *Modernity at Large: Cultural Dimensions of Globalisation*
Philippe Ariès's *Centuries of Childhood*
Franz Boas's *Race, Language and Culture*
Kim Chan & Renée Mauborgne's *Blue Ocean Strategy*
Jared Diamond's *Guns, Germs & Steel: the Fate of Human Societies*
Jared Diamond's *Collapse: How Societies Choose to Fail or Survive*
E. E. Evans-Pritchard's *Witchcraft, Oracles and Magic Among the Azande*
James Ferguson's *The Anti-Politics Machine*
Clifford Geertz's *The Interpretation of Cultures*
David Graeber's *Debt: the First 5000 Years*
Karen Ho's *Liquidated: An Ethnography of Wall Street*
Geert Hofstede's *Culture's Consequences: Comparing Values, Behaviors, Institutes and Organizations across Nations*
Claude Lévi-Strauss's *Structural Anthropology*
Jay Macleod's *Ain't No Makin' It: Aspirations and Attainment in a Low-Income Neighborhood*
Saba Mahmood's *The Politics of Piety: The Islamic Revival and the Feminist Subjec*t
Marcel Mauss's *The Gift*

BUSINESS

Jean Lave & Etienne Wenger's *Situated Learning*
Theodore Levitt's *Marketing Myopia*
Burton G. Malkiel's *A Random Walk Down Wall Street*
Douglas McGregor's *The Human Side of Enterprise*
Michael Porter's *Competitive Strategy: Creating and Sustaining Superior Performance*
John Kotter's *Leading Change*
C. K. Prahalad & Gary Hamel's *The Core Competence of the Corporation*

CRIMINOLOGY

Michelle Alexander's *The New Jim Crow: Mass Incarceration in the Age of Colorblindness*
Michael R. Gottfredson & Travis Hirschi's *A General Theory of Crime*
Richard Herrnstein & Charles A. Murray's *The Bell Curve: Intelligence and Class Structure in American Life*
Elizabeth Loftus's *Eyewitness Testimony*
Jay Macleod's *Ain't No Makin' It: Aspirations and Attainment in a Low-Income Neighborhood*
Philip Zimbardo's *The Lucifer Effect*

ECONOMICS

Janet Abu-Lughod's *Before European Hegemony*
Ha-Joon Chang's *Kicking Away the Ladder*
David Brion Davis's *The Problem of Slavery in the Age of Revolution*
Milton Friedman's *The Role of Monetary Policy*
Milton Friedman's *Capitalism and Freedom*
David Graeber's *Debt: the First 5000 Years*
Friedrich Hayek's *The Road to Serfdom*
Karen Ho's *Liquidated: An Ethnography of Wall Street*

John Maynard Keynes's *The General Theory of Employment, Interest and Money*
Charles P. Kindleberger's *Manias, Panics and Crashes*
Robert Lucas's *Why Doesn't Capital Flow from Rich to Poor Countries?*
Burton G. Malkiel's *A Random Walk Down Wall Street*
Thomas Robert Malthus's *An Essay on the Principle of Population*
Karl Marx's *Capital*
Thomas Piketty's *Capital in the Twenty-First Century*
Amartya Sen's *Development as Freedom*
Adam Smith's *The Wealth of Nations*
Nassim Nicholas Taleb's *The Black Swan: The Impact of the Highly Improbable*
Amos Tversky's & Daniel Kahneman's *Judgment under Uncertainty: Heuristics and Biases*
Mahbub Ul Haq's *Reflections on Human Development*
Max Weber's *The Protestant Ethic and the Spirit of Capitalism*

FEMINISM AND GENDER STUDIES

Judith Butler's *Gender Trouble*
Simone De Beauvoir's *The Second Sex*
Michel Foucault's *History of Sexuality*
Betty Friedan's *The Feminine Mystique*
Saba Mahmood's *The Politics of Piety: The Islamic Revival and the Feminist Subject*
Joan Wallach Scott's *Gender and the Politics of History*
Mary Wollstonecraft's *A Vindication of the Rights of Woman*
Virginia Woolf's *A Room of One's Own*

GEOGRAPHY

The Brundtland Report's *Our Common Future*
Rachel Carson's *Silent Spring*
Charles Darwin's *On the Origin of Species*
James Ferguson's *The Anti-Politics Machine*
Jane Jacobs's *The Death and Life of Great American Cities*
James Lovelock's *Gaia: A New Look at Life on Earth*
Amartya Sen's *Development as Freedom*
Mathis Wackernagel & William Rees's *Our Ecological Footprint*

HISTORY

Janet Abu-Lughod's *Before European Hegemony*
Benedict Anderson's *Imagined Communities*
Bernard Bailyn's *The Ideological Origins of the American Revolution*
Hanna Batatu's *The Old Social Classes And The Revolutionary Movements Of Iraq*
Christopher Browning's *Ordinary Men: Reserve Police Batallion 101 and the Final Solution in Poland*
Edmund Burke's *Reflections on the Revolution in France*
William Cronon's *Nature's Metropolis: Chicago And The Great West*
Alfred W. Crosby's *The Columbian Exchange*
Hamid Dabashi's *Iran: A People Interrupted*
David Brion Davis's *The Problem of Slavery in the Age of Revolution*
Nathalie Zemon Davis's *The Return of Martin Guerre*
Jared Diamond's *Guns, Germs & Steel: the Fate of Human Societies*
Frank Dikotter's *Mao's Great Famine*
John W Dower's *War Without Mercy: Race And Power In The Pacific War*
W. E. B. Du Bois's *The Souls of Black Folk*
Richard J. Evans's *In Defence of History*
Lucien Febvre's *The Problem of Unbelief in the 16th Century*
Sheila Fitzpatrick's *Everyday Stalinism*

The Macat Library By Discipline

Eric Foner's *Reconstruction: America's Unfinished Revolution, 1863-1877*
Michel Foucault's *Discipline and Punish*
Michel Foucault's *History of Sexuality*
Francis Fukuyama's *The End of History and the Last Man*
John Lewis Gaddis's *We Now Know: Rethinking Cold War History*
Ernest Gellner's *Nations and Nationalism*
Eugene Genovese's *Roll, Jordan, Roll: The World the Slaves Made*
Carlo Ginzburg's *The Night Battles*
Daniel Goldhagen's *Hitler's Willing Executioners*
Jack Goldstone's *Revolution and Rebellion in the Early Modern World*
Antonio Gramsci's *The Prison Notebooks*
Alexander Hamilton, John Jay & James Madison's *The Federalist Papers*
Christopher Hill's *The World Turned Upside Down*
Carole Hillenbrand's *The Crusades: Islamic Perspectives*
Thomas Hobbes's *Leviathan*
Eric Hobsbawm's *The Age Of Revolution*
John A. Hobson's *Imperialism: A Study*
Albert Hourani's *History of the Arab Peoples*
Samuel P. Huntington's *The Clash of Civilizations and the Remaking of World Order*
C. L. R. James's *The Black Jacobins*
Tony Judt's *Postwar: A History of Europe Since 1945*
Ernst Kantorowicz's *The King's Two Bodies: A Study in Medieval Political Theology*
Paul Kennedy's *The Rise and Fall of the Great Powers*
Ian Kershaw's *The "Hitler Myth": Image and Reality in the Third Reich*
John Maynard Keynes's *The General Theory of Employment, Interest and Money*
Charles P. Kindleberger's *Manias, Panics and Crashes*
Martin Luther King Jr's *Why We Can't Wait*
Henry Kissinger's *World Order: Reflections on the Character of Nations and the Course of History*
Thomas Kuhn's *The Structure of Scientific Revolutions*
Georges Lefebvre's *The Coming of the French Revolution*
John Locke's *Two Treatises of Government*
Niccolò Machiavelli's *The Prince*
Thomas Robert Malthus's *An Essay on the Principle of Population*
Mahmood Mamdani's *Citizen and Subject: Contemporary Africa And The Legacy Of Late Colonialism*
Karl Marx's *Capital*
Stanley Milgram's *Obedience to Authority*
John Stuart Mill's *On Liberty*
Thomas Paine's *Common Sense*
Thomas Paine's *Rights of Man*
Geoffrey Parker's *Global Crisis: War, Climate Change and Catastrophe in the Seventeenth Century*
Jonathan Riley-Smith's *The First Crusade and the Idea of Crusading*
Jean-Jacques Rousseau's *The Social Contract*
Joan Wallach Scott's *Gender and the Politics of History*
Theda Skocpol's *States and Social Revolutions*
Adam Smith's *The Wealth of Nations*
Timothy Snyder's *Bloodlands: Europe Between Hitler and Stalin*
Sun Tzu's *The Art of War*
Keith Thomas's *Religion and the Decline of Magic*
Thucydides's *The History of the Peloponnesian War*
Frederick Jackson Turner's *The Significance of the Frontier in American History*
Odd Arne Westad's *The Global Cold War: Third World Interventions And The Making Of Our Times*

LITERATURE

Chinua Achebe's *An Image of Africa: Racism in Conrad's Heart of Darkness*
Roland Barthes's *Mythologies*
Homi K. Bhabha's *The Location of Culture*
Judith Butler's *Gender Trouble*
Simone De Beauvoir's *The Second Sex*
Ferdinand De Saussure's *Course in General Linguistics*
T. S. Eliot's *The Sacred Wood: Essays on Poetry and Criticism*
Zora Neale Huston's *Characteristics of Negro Expression*
Toni Morrison's *Playing in the Dark: Whiteness in the American Literary Imagination*
Edward Said's *Orientalism*
Gayatri Chakravorty Spivak's *Can the Subaltern Speak?*
Mary Wollstonecraft's *A Vindication of the Rights of Women*
Virginia Woolf's *A Room of One's Own*

PHILOSOPHY

Elizabeth Anscombe's *Modern Moral Philosophy*
Hannah Arendt's *The Human Condition*
Aristotle's *Metaphysics*
Aristotle's *Nicomachean Ethics*
Edmund Gettier's *Is Justified True Belief Knowledge?*
Georg Wilhelm Friedrich Hegel's *Phenomenology of Spirit*
David Hume's *Dialogues Concerning Natural Religion*
David Hume's *The Enquiry for Human Understanding*
Immanuel Kant's *Religion within the Boundaries of Mere Reason*
Immanuel Kant's *Critique of Pure Reason*
Søren Kierkegaard's *The Sickness Unto Death*
Søren Kierkegaard's *Fear and Trembling*
C. S. Lewis's *The Abolition of Man*
Alasdair MacIntyre's *After Virtue*
Marcus Aurelius's *Meditations*
Friedrich Nietzsche's *On the Genealogy of Morality*
Friedrich Nietzsche's *Beyond Good and Evil*
Plato's *Republic*
Plato's *Symposium*
Jean-Jacques Rousseau's *The Social Contract*
Gilbert Ryle's *The Concept of Mind*
Baruch Spinoza's *Ethics*
Sun Tzu's *The Art of War*
Ludwig Wittgenstein's *Philosophical Investigations*

POLITICS

Benedict Anderson's *Imagined Communities*
Aristotle's *Politics*
Bernard Bailyn's *The Ideological Origins of the American Revolution*
Edmund Burke's *Reflections on the Revolution in France*
John C. Calhoun's *A Disquisition on Government*
Ha-Joon Chang's *Kicking Away the Ladder*
Hamid Dabashi's *Iran: A People Interrupted*
Hamid Dabashi's *Theology of Discontent: The Ideological Foundation of the Islamic Revolution in Iran*
Robert Dahl's *Democracy and its Critics*
Robert Dahl's *Who Governs?*
David Brion Davis's *The Problem of Slavery in the Age of Revolution*

The Macat Library By Discipline

Alexis De Tocqueville's *Democracy in America*
James Ferguson's *The Anti-Politics Machine*
Frank Dikotter's *Mao's Great Famine*
Sheila Fitzpatrick's *Everyday Stalinism*
Eric Foner's *Reconstruction: America's Unfinished Revolution, 1863-1877*
Milton Friedman's *Capitalism and Freedom*
Francis Fukuyama's *The End of History and the Last Man*
John Lewis Gaddis's *We Now Know: Rethinking Cold War History*
Ernest Gellner's *Nations and Nationalism*
David Graeber's *Debt: the First 5000 Years*
Antonio Gramsci's *The Prison Notebooks*
Alexander Hamilton, John Jay & James Madison's *The Federalist Papers*
Friedrich Hayek's *The Road to Serfdom*
Christopher Hill's *The World Turned Upside Down*
Thomas Hobbes's *Leviathan*
John A. Hobson's *Imperialism: A Study*
Samuel P. Huntington's *The Clash of Civilizations and the Remaking of World Order*
Tony Judt's *Postwar: A History of Europe Since 1945*
David C. Kang's *China Rising: Peace, Power and Order in East Asia*
Paul Kennedy's *The Rise and Fall of Great Powers*
Robert Keohane's *After Hegemony*
Martin Luther King Jr.'s *Why We Can't Wait*
Henry Kissinger's *World Order: Reflections on the Character of Nations and the Course of History*
John Locke's *Two Treatises of Government*
Niccolò Machiavelli's *The Prince*
Thomas Robert Malthus's *An Essay on the Principle of Population*
Mahmood Mamdani's *Citizen and Subject: Contemporary Africa And The Legacy Of Late Colonialism*
Karl Marx's *Capital*
John Stuart Mill's *On Liberty*
John Stuart Mill's *Utilitarianism*
Hans Morgenthau's *Politics Among Nations*
Thomas Paine's *Common Sense*
Thomas Paine's *Rights of Man*
Thomas Piketty's *Capital in the Twenty-First Century*
Robert D. Putman's *Bowling Alone*
John Rawls's *Theory of Justice*
Jean-Jacques Rousseau's *The Social Contract*
Theda Skocpol's *States and Social Revolutions*
Adam Smith's *The Wealth of Nations*
Sun Tzu's *The Art of War*
Henry David Thoreau's *Civil Disobedience*
Thucydides's *The History of the Peloponnesian War*
Kenneth Waltz's *Theory of International Politics*
Max Weber's *Politics as a Vocation*
Odd Arne Westad's *The Global Cold War: Third World Interventions And The Making Of Our Times*

POSTCOLONIAL STUDIES

Roland Barthes's *Mythologies*
Frantz Fanon's *Black Skin, White Masks*
Homi K. Bhabha's *The Location of Culture*
Gustavo Gutiérrez's *A Theology of Liberation*
Edward Said's *Orientalism*
Gayatri Chakravorty Spivak's *Can the Subaltern Speak?*

PSYCHOLOGY

Gordon Allport's *The Nature of Prejudice*
Alan Baddeley & Graham Hitch's *Aggression: A Social Learning Analysis*
Albert Bandura's *Aggression: A Social Learning Analysis*
Leon Festinger's *A Theory of Cognitive Dissonance*
Sigmund Freud's *The Interpretation of Dreams*
Betty Friedan's *The Feminine Mystique*
Michael R. Gottfredson & Travis Hirschi's *A General Theory of Crime*
Eric Hoffer's *The True Believer: Thoughts on the Nature of Mass Movements*
William James's *Principles of Psychology*
Elizabeth Loftus's *Eyewitness Testimony*
A. H. Maslow's *A Theory of Human Motivation*
Stanley Milgram's *Obedience to Authority*
Steven Pinker's *The Better Angels of Our Nature*
Oliver Sacks's *The Man Who Mistook His Wife For a Hat*
Richard Thaler & Cass Sunstein's *Nudge: Improving Decisions About Health, Wealth and Happiness*
Amos Tversky's *Judgment under Uncertainty: Heuristics and Biases*
Philip Zimbardo's *The Lucifer Effect*

SCIENCE

Rachel Carson's *Silent Spring*
William Cronon's *Nature's Metropolis: Chicago And The Great West*
Alfred W. Crosby's *The Columbian Exchange*
Charles Darwin's *On the Origin of Species*
Richard Dawkin's *The Selfish Gene*
Thomas Kuhn's *The Structure of Scientific Revolutions*
Geoffrey Parker's *Global Crisis: War, Climate Change and Catastrophe in the Seventeenth Century*
Mathis Wackernagel & William Rees's *Our Ecological Footprint*

SOCIOLOGY

Michelle Alexander's *The New Jim Crow: Mass Incarceration in the Age of Colorblindness*
Gordon Allport's *The Nature of Prejudice*
Albert Bandura's *Aggression: A Social Learning Analysis*
Hanna Batatu's *The Old Social Classes And The Revolutionary Movements Of Iraq*
Ha-Joon Chang's *Kicking Away the Ladder*
W. E. B. Du Bois's *The Souls of Black Folk*
Émile Durkheim's *On Suicide*
Frantz Fanon's *Black Skin, White Masks*
Frantz Fanon's *The Wretched of the Earth*
Eric Foner's *Reconstruction: America's Unfinished Revolution, 1863-1877*
Eugene Genovese's *Roll, Jordan, Roll: The World the Slaves Made*
Jack Goldstone's *Revolution and Rebellion in the Early Modern World*
Antonio Gramsci's *The Prison Notebooks*
Richard Herrnstein & Charles A Murray's *The Bell Curve: Intelligence and Class Structure in American Life*
Eric Hoffer's *The True Believer: Thoughts on the Nature of Mass Movements*
Jane Jacobs's *The Death and Life of Great American Cities*
Robert Lucas's *Why Doesn't Capital Flow from Rich to Poor Countries?*
Jay Macleod's *Ain't No Makin' It: Aspirations and Attainment in a Low Income Neighborhood*
Elaine May's *Homeward Bound: American Families in the Cold War Era*
Douglas McGregor's *The Human Side of Enterprise*
C. Wright Mills's *The Sociological Imagination*

The Macat Library By Discipline

Thomas Piketty's *Capital in the Twenty-First Century*
Robert D. Putman's *Bowling Alone*
David Riesman's *The Lonely Crowd: A Study of the Changing American Character*
Edward Said's *Orientalism*
Joan Wallach Scott's *Gender and the Politics of History*
Theda Skocpol's *States and Social Revolutions*
Max Weber's *The Protestant Ethic and the Spirit of Capitalism*

THEOLOGY

Augustine's *Confessions*
Benedict's *Rule of St Benedict*
Gustavo Gutiérrez's *A Theology of Liberation*
Carole Hillenbrand's *The Crusades: Islamic Perspectives*
David Hume's *Dialogues Concerning Natural Religion*
Immanuel Kant's *Religion within the Boundaries of Mere Reason*
Ernst Kantorowicz's *The King's Two Bodies: A Study in Medieval Political Theology*
Søren Kierkegaard's *The Sickness Unto Death*
C. S. Lewis's *The Abolition of Man*
Saba Mahmood's *The Politics of Piety: The Islamic Revival and the Feminist Subject*
Baruch Spinoza's *Ethics*
Keith Thomas's *Religion and the Decline of Magic*

COMING SOON

Chris Argyris's *The Individual and the Organisation*
Seyla Benhabib's *The Rights of Others*
Walter Benjamin's *The Work Of Art in the Age of Mechanical Reproduction*
John Berger's *Ways of Seeing*
Pierre Bourdieu's *Outline of a Theory of Practice*
Mary Douglas's *Purity and Danger*
Roland Dworkin's *Taking Rights Seriously*
James G. March's *Exploration and Exploitation in Organisational Learning*
Ikujiro Nonaka's *A Dynamic Theory of Organizational Knowledge Creation*
Griselda Pollock's *Vision and Difference*
Amartya Sen's *Inequality Re-Examined*
Susan Sontag's *On Photography*
Yasser Tabbaa's *The Transformation of Islamic Art*
Ludwig von Mises's *Theory of Money and Credit*

Macat Disciplines

Access the greatest ideas and thinkers across entire disciplines, including

FEMINISM, GENDER AND QUEER STUDIES

Simone De Beauvoir's
The Second Sex

Michel Foucault's
History of Sexuality

Betty Friedan's
The Feminine Mystique

Saba Mahmood's
*The Politics of Piety:
The Islamic Revival and
the Feminist Subject*

Joan Wallach Scott's
*Gender and the
Politics of History*

Mary Wollstonecraft's
*A Vindication of the
Rights of Woman*

Virginia Woolf's
A Room of One's Own

Judith Butler's
Gender Trouble

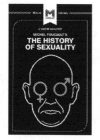

Macat Disciplines

Access the greatest ideas and thinkers across entire disciplines, including

INEQUALITY

Ha-Joon Chang's, *Kicking Away the Ladder*

David Graeber's, *Debt: The First 5000 Years*

Robert E. Lucas's, *Why Doesn't Capital Flow from Rich To Poor Countries?*

Thomas Piketty's, *Capital in the Twenty-First Century*

Amartya Sen's, *Inequality Re-Examined*

Mahbub Ul Haq's, *Reflections on Human Development*

Macat analyses are available from all good bookshops and libraries.

Access hundreds of analyses through one, multimedia tool.

Join free for one month **library.macat.com**

Macat Disciplines

Access the greatest ideas and thinkers across entire disciplines, including

CRIMINOLOGY

Michelle Alexander's
*The New Jim Crow:
Mass Incarceration in the
Age of Colorblindness*

**Michael R. Gottfredson
& Travis Hirschi's**
A General Theory of Crime

Elizabeth Loftus's
Eyewitness Testimony

**Richard Herrnstein
& Charles A. Murray's**
*The Bell Curve: Intelligence and
Class Structure in American Life*

Jay Macleod's
*Ain't No Makin' It:
Aspirations and Attainment in a
Low-Income Neighborhood*

Philip Zimbardo's
The Lucifer Effect

Macat Disciplines

Access the greatest ideas and thinkers across entire disciplines, including

Postcolonial Studies

Roland Barthes's *Mythologies*
Frantz Fanon's *Black Skin, White Masks*
Homi K. Bhabha's *The Location of Culture*
Gustavo Gutiérrez's *A Theology of Liberation*
Edward Said's *Orientalism*
Gayatri Chakravorty Spivak's *Can the Subaltern Speak?*

Macat Pairs

Analyse historical and modern issues from opposite sides of an argument. Pairs include:

HOW TO RUN AN ECONOMY

John Maynard Keynes's
The General Theory OF Employment, Interest and Money

Classical economics suggests that market economies are self-correcting in times of recession or depression, and tend toward full employment and output. But English economist John Maynard Keynes disagrees.

In his ground-breaking 1936 study *The General Theory*, Keynes argues that traditional economics has misunderstood the causes of unemployment. Employment is not determined by the price of labor; it is directly linked to demand. Keynes believes market economies are by nature unstable, and so require government intervention. Spurred on by the social catastrophe of the Great Depression of the 1930s, he sets out to revolutionize the way the world thinks

Milton Friedman's
The Role of Monetary Policy

Friedman's 1968 paper changed the course of economic theory. In just 17 pages, he demolished existing theory and outlined an effective alternate monetary policy designed to secure 'high employment, stable prices and rapid growth.'

Friedman demonstrated that monetary policy plays a vital role in broader economic stability and argued that economists got their monetary policy wrong in the 1950s and 1960s by misunderstanding the relationship between inflation and unemployment. Previous generations of economists had believed that governments could permanently decrease unemployment by permitting inflation—and vice versa. Friedman's most original contribution was to show that this supposed trade-off is an illusion that only works in the short term.

Macat analyses are available from all good bookshops and libraries.

Access hundreds of analyses through one, multimedia tool.
Join free for one month **library.macat.com**

Macat Disciplines

*Access the greatest ideas and thinkers
across entire disciplines, including*

THE FUTURE OF DEMOCRACY

Robert A. Dahl's, *Democracy and Its Critics*
Robert A. Dahl's, *Who Governs?*
Alexis De Toqueville's, *Democracy in America*
Niccolò Machiavelli's, *The Prince*
John Stuart Mill's, *On Liberty*
Robert D. Putnam's, *Bowling Alone*
Jean-Jacques Rousseau's, *The Social Contract*
Henry David Thoreau's, *Civil Disobedience*

Macat Disciplines

Access the greatest ideas and thinkers across entire disciplines, including

TOTALITARIANISM

Sheila Fitzpatrick's, *Everyday Stalinism*
Ian Kershaw's, *The "Hitler Myth"*
Timothy Snyder's, *Bloodlands*

Printed in the United States
by Baker & Taylor Publisher Services